LEVEL UP LEADERSHIP: ADVANCE YOUR EDUGAME

Brian Kulak

Level Up Leadership
Brian Kulak

Published by EduMatch®
PO Box 150324, Alexandria, VA 22315
www.edumatch.org

These books are available at special
discounts when purchased in quantities of 10
or more for use as premiums, promotions
fundraising, and educational use. For
inquiries and details, contact the publisher:
sarah@edumatch.org.

DEDICATION

Though always in the back of my mind, writing a book seemed perpetually out of reach, a tantalizing item on a too tall shelf. Thanks to the people mentioned herein, that item kept getting closer and closer until I could take it off the shelf and claim it as my own.

To my wife, who supported me by providing kid-free time to focus, write, edit, and promote. To my daughter, whose curiosity, creativity, and empathy inspire me to level up every day. To my son, who pushed start on a game of *Super Mario Brothers* and inspired me to push start on this book. They are the period at the end of all my sentences.

To my parents, who read my childhood tales of time travel and sports with equal parts pride and confusion. And to my Aunt Beth, who shared her own writing with me when I was a child and provided me with a writing role model.

To Sue Anderson, Beth Canzanese, Lisa McGilloway, and John Skrabonja, who represent four stars in my leadership constellation. Sue was the first teacher to encourage my creative writing, Lisa challenged me to be a better writer, John taught me how to teach, and Beth helped guide my path regardless of where it took me.

To Kaylee Collins, Dylan Fenton, Rob Kuestner, Jennifer McPartland, and Anna Muessig, who gave up time with family and friends to read my draft and provide me with invaluable feedback.

To Scott Oswald, the best leader with whom I have ever worked and whom I want to be when I grow up.

To Karen Draper, my therapist, who introduced me to myself seven years ago. Without her, no book would have been written.

To Dan Whalen and Rich Czyz, two dudes whose infectious positivity and selfless kindness paved the way for me to get out of my own way and finally bring *Level Up Leadership* to life.

To my former students, who remain friends, teammates, guest bloggers, and silly text thread participants.

To Joe Levine and Rob Stewart at CC&G, Inc, who graciously agreed to set up my blog. To Brian Hogan, whose vision and creativity brought my logo and book cover to life.

To my EduMatch family of writers, especially the inimitable Sarah Thomas and Mandy Froehlich, two women whose fingerprints are all over this book. To Judy Arzt, whose editing humbled and motivated me, even if I may/might never know how to use may/might properly.

Thank you, all.

CONTENTS

FOREWORD

It all began with a simple email. An administrator from a neighboring district wanted to pick my brain about a couple of topics. All for conversation about topics that I am passionate about, I welcomed Brian Kulak to come visit me at my school. After finally being able to coordinate our schedules, we were going to meet in our school's conference room, and I wasn't sure exactly what to expect. Brian wanted to touch base to pick my brain about my writing process.

When the day finally arrived, it was as if we had known each other for years. We talked about my writing process. We talked about what Brian was trying to accomplish with his own writing process. We talked about education, and how we can be successful in schools, and why some things don't work out in schools. Almost two full hours just melted away.

At the end of the meeting, we promised to keep in touch. And I realized that I had a kindred spirit. Someone who was in a similar position to me and understood exactly what I am trying to accomplish, and me him. As our friendship has grown, we've discovered that we are passionate about a lot of topics...

- Baseball...
- 90's Music, particularly the Seattle scene...
- A Tribe Called Quest...
- Moving education forward...
- And Video Games.

It's these last two that Brian has combined in order to Level Up Leadership. At our initial meeting, when Brian began describing the idea behind this book, I was intrigued. I would have considered myself a video game aficionado when I was younger, but hadn't played in many years. When he began to compare our journey as educators with the plight of Super Mario, I was instantly hooked. I started playing games again. It took me back to my youth, and made me think about the connections between these fantasy worlds and our own complex daily lives.

I began to ponder:

What is it about video games that draws us in, that forces us to blow up the outside world for hours at a time, sometimes to save a princess, sometimes to quarterback an NFL team, sometimes just to organize a bunch of blocks?

And I realized, it's all about goals. Setting your goal. Working nonstop to achieve that goal. Improving upon your goal. Finding the resources that will help you meet your goal. Using cheat codes that give you more lives to improve your chances. Being so focused and ultimately driven by your goal, that you want nothing more than to be successful. And once you are successful with your goal, you don't just stop, you push on. You settle on a new goal and repeat the process. You move forward (usually to the right) and you continue moving forward no matter what.

It's the same in education, you set your goal. You do everything in your power to accomplish it. You find those physical and human resources who can help you in your quest. Once you achieve your goal, you improve upon it, and continue to move forward no matter what.

When Brian initially shared his idea for this book, I was *Super* excited. Brian shared that his goal was to write every day, no matter what. He began to write, relied on the resources that he found, and pushed to his goal with a feverish excitement and determination, that we sometimes see only when someone is about to conquer that video game world that they've been working on for months. As I've come to know Brian over these past couple of years, I've realized that it's all about goals. Set your goal. Fall. Get back up. Repeat. Continue to improve and push forward no matter what.

The fantasy video game worlds that we inhabit are much like the classrooms and schools that we inhabit. It's time that we all set our goal to Level Up Leadership. It's time that we play our game, find those resources, and Level Up what we are doing for kids every day.

Live by a simple mantra, one that has worked for Brian, and so many others...

WWSMD?

What would **Super Mario** do?

Like Brian, he wouldn't give up on his goal, and neither should you. It's time to get going right now. Level Up and don't look back!

Rich Czyz
Educator and Author, *The Four O'Clock Faculty*

INTRODUCTION

For generations, video games have provided players with endless hours of entertainment, frustration, puzzles, and bosses. From *Pong* ("Pong") to *Pac-Man* ("Pac-Man"), from *Super Mario Brothers* ("Super Mario Brothers") to *Tomb Raider* ("Tomb Raider"), and from *Madden NFL* ("Madden NFL") to *Minecraft* ("Minecraft"), we have made conscious decisions to enter into worlds knowing full well in some cases there is no "end"; in other cases, we have had to "die" countless times before achieving anything, and in still other cases, we have had to reference a walkthrough to guide our way.

A small segment of players might have even decided to quit if the game proves too challenging.

Video game evolution became part of our national zeitgeist in the 1980s, when nary a pizza shop or dentist's office waiting room was complete without some blinking, beeping monstrosity daring us to enter a quarter and try our luck. Entire weekends were planned around heading to the local arcade to try to etch our digital initials into that pantheon of gaming immorality known as the high scoreboard. Eventually, home gaming systems allowed us to compete at home, without quarters, against our friends, family, or even the CPU itself in a quest for those high scores or, in many cases, bragging rights. More recently, gaming has become a billion-dollar industry replete with undergraduate programs dedicated to its design, televised tournaments headlined by bankrolled players, website and television shows dedicated to its prominence, and a culture of gamers with fans not unlike rock stars or athletes.

Akin to any video game is the gamer's often obsessive desire to win. Complex puzzle solving, on-demand decision making, hand-eye-coordination, and time management all afford gamers with the opportunity to save the princess, recover the lost artifact, or send those pesky evil spirits back from whence they came. In any of those scenarios, players are wholly aware that the player, character, or avatar with which they begin the game is rarely, if ever, the same by game's end.

You see in order to win any game, it is imperative for the player to "level up."

Arguably, the most revered video game character is Mario from the Mario Brothers franchise (note: Mario's full name must be Mario Mario if he and his brother Luigi are the Mario Brothers, right? Weird). In the most recognizable incarnation, *Super Mario Brothers*, Mario is on a perpetual mission to free and reunite with Princess Toadstool. Since the game's release in 1985, Mario has existed in dozens of worlds, as part of several consoles, and in the hands of multiple generations under the same roof. However, once we hit the start button to begin Mario's adventure, we see an undersized, if not spunky, outnumbered, and unlikely hero ready to save his beloved.

Quickly, we realize that through ingenuity and, in some cases, luck, Mario can actually "level up." Hit a brick square or a floating question mark, and he will grow and eventually be granted with the ability to throw fireballs at his enemies. Because he's leveled up, the path to his beloved princess should be considerably easier. While such improvements to Mario's size and physical capabilities are helpful, neither accounts for a constantly undulating world of floating and often disappearing platforms, unpredictable pitfalls and enemies, and a rapidly ticking timer counting down to his inevitable death. What's worse is that Mario's margin of error is so small, that a singular misstep can strip him of his power or, worse, send him to his digital demise.

So, while having the ability to squash enemies by jumping on their heads or to incinerate them with his fireballs is nice, Mario is still Mario, the diminutive, lovesick plumber willing to do whatever it takes to succeed. As his human surrogate, we travel on his journey and feel what we can only assume he feels because we are, ultimately, responsible for his success or failure. In this way, we are all Mario.

While watching my five-year-old play *Super Mario Brothers* on his new, old-school Nintendo, I began to draw parallels between gaming and education. As he jumped, dodged, and giggled his way through a series of failures (he rarely gets past level 1-2), I started to view the game as a functional analogy for our lives as educators. We, too, are beset by a constantly changing landscape; we, too, have to fail forward as many times as it takes before we learn from our mistakes and grow into better teachers and leaders; we, too, have no shortage of pitfalls and distractions aimed at keeping us from our goals; and we, too, have every opportunity to level up on the way to a career filled with empathy, passion, and pride. We might not have gold coins to collect or a princess to save, but we do have a mission, like Mario, that is deeply personal and intensely gratifying.

But watching my son play wasn't enough. Because of his limited skillset and tsetse-fly-attention-span, I couldn't get the full scope of how Mario's journey mirrors our own. So I did what any former gamer would do: I played. I played before work, I played after I put the kids to bed, I played at halftime of the Eagles game on Sunday, I played whenever I could. Thanks to the Nintendo Mini's ("Nintendo Entertainment System: NES Classic") save feature, itself unheard of at the dawn of Nintendo gaming, I could play in short spurts and then return to real life. I would push pause ad nauseum so I could take notes. I'd read about each level before and after I played, so I knew what to expect and to make sure I didn't miss anything. What once was a gaming approach based on reckless abandon became a surgical procedure. I wasn't trying to beat the game; I was trying to understand the game.

Together, we'll explore how video game tropes can help us better frame our teaching and leadership. By analogizing our work as educational leaders, we can approach such work from a lens foreign from, but oddly similar to, our own. In effect, we will begin to level up our leadership in such a way that allows us to predict the disappearing floorboard, to seek that necessary Easter egg even if it takes us out of our way, and to constantly reinvent ourselves on the way to reuniting with our own Princess Toadstool.

Player 1 Push Start.

1

LEVEL ONE

When we first meet Mario, he is a stranger in a strange land. He is oddly miniature and dressed in some kind of workmanlike onesie complete with his signature red hat, and he is only vaguely aware of the direction in which he must travel, right, to save the princess. Pleasant, if not repetitive, music drones on as he takes those first tentative steps toward achieving his goal. What's more is that a visible timer ticks down ominously fast, perpetually reminding Mario that even saving a kidnapped princess has to meet a certain prescribed standard of bureaucratic choosing.

Within his first few tentative steps, Mario is greeted by a floating platform imprinted with a question mark. Acclimating immediately to his new surroundings, Mario realizes he can jump and bonk the question mark to release a gold coin. Such incentive-based decisions are rife throughout the game. In fact, accumulating 100 coins earns Mario a highly coveted extra life.

Almost simultaneously, he is met by the first of countless obstacles meant to distract, confuse, or defeat Mario before he can be reunited with his sweetheart. This first incarnation is a scowling mini-mushroom, called a Goomba, on a collision course with our hero. Luckily, this low-level minion is only programmed to walk in a straight line, do what it's told (destroy Mario), and fall in line. Some quick thinking allows Mario to simply jump on the wayward mushroom's head, thereby squashing it and ostensibly sending it back to whatever hellscape in which it was spawned. Unfortunately, the Goomba is Mario's most common enemy, the kind with which he will have to deal throughout his journey.

Now back to those floating games of chance. More often than not, jumping into a question mark will, in fact, elicit a gold coin. However, the powers that be have also seen fit to provide Mario with some much-needed support during his journey. Coming in four forms, a red and yellow mushroom, a blazing flower, a spritely blinking star, or a green and yellow mushroom, each makes Mario stronger or provides him with an extra life. In this case, if Mario ingests the red and yellow mushroom he frees from a floating question mark, he'll be made significantly larger, a welcome change from his original size. As a result, such growth allows for Mario to absorb extra contact from a baddie, thereby making his journey a bit more manageable.

Equally important are the suspended brick squares peppered throughout the game. Like the question mark structures, Mario is able to nudge these when he's small (or bash them when he's on steroids), in hopes that they, too, will provide him with a helpful surprise. Often they do not, but sometimes Mario can find a trove of coins or a power-up inside these bricks.

The choice, however, is his. Certainly, he can choose to ignore the possibility for improvement in favor of a more efficient, hardline approach to heroism.

Shortly thereafter, Mario is granted with a glowing flower, which grants him the ability to generate and throw fireballs at his unsuspecting enemies. Again, though, Mario has to decide to activate the flower by bonking the question mark in which it resides. Soon, Mario is met by his next adversary, a paradoxically happy turtle, called a Koopa Troopa. Unlike its dimwitted mushroom brethren, the Troopa is slightly stronger and can be vanquished by a fireball or by jumping on its shell and then kicking it off-screen. Luckily, just as the Goombas and Troopas are increasing their ranks, Mario is granted another power-up, the blinking star, which makes him temporarily invincible. Typically, players will speed through the level while on this high, running roughshod over any enemy that gets in Mario's way. Mario feels empowered in a way he never has before, and though fleeting, he often does his best work in this altered state.

Finally, a well-timed jump at a seemingly random time produces an invisible platform inside of which are the often-elusive extra life mushrooms. Collecting these takes time, patience, and risk, but stockpiling extra lives proves necessary as Mario's journey gets increasingly difficult. Speaking of time, Mario is presented, on almost every level, with the tantalizing prospect of a shortcut. Through an intricate system of pipes built into each level, Mario can descend into a coin-filled sewer of sorts, collect those coins, and then ascend to the surface at a point much farther along than he would have been, had he just stayed the course. Consider, too, that choosing the shortcut means being unable to return to areas he otherwise would have explored on the surface, thereby missing out on whatever adventures or power-ups might have been available.

Finally, Mario reaches the end of the level, which ends, as most do, with a triumphant leap onto a high flagpole adorned with a peace-sign flag. Mario is rewarded, in points, for the length and height of his jump as well as for his time to complete the level. He slides down the flagpole, and he enters a small, brick castle as his hero's theme song plays.

To the untrained eye, the parallels between video games and leadership seem a stretch.

But like gaming, whose evolution has been at warp speed since its inception, how we lead is rooted in purpose (saving the princess), passion (our hero's love for the princess), strategy (deciding the best possible way to approach each mission), bosses (those meant to keep us from the princess), and reflection (accepting that it might take hundreds of tries before we are able to move on). In order for us to save our proverbial princess, we have to, like Mario, find ways to support our mission despite the increasingly difficult terrain, the inevitable pitfalls--both seen and unseen--and the ne'er-do-wells who stand in our way.

Level Up Leadership
Brian Kulak

Gamer's Journal: I've been through exactly three level 1s in my twenty years in education: as a 22-year old, first-year teacher; as a 36-year old, first-year Chief Academic Officer; and as a 41-year old first-year principal. In each, I had relatively no idea what I was doing. And I knew it. However, like Mario, in each iteration I was convinced that I was on a singular mission regardless of how outmatched I was.

My first year in the classroom was marked by lessons that ran too short or too long, lectures that were too collegiate, too wordy, too teacher-centric, and assessments that were, plainly, weak. To offset such abject averageness, I had to level up. I got creative with lesson design, I got students talking and listening, and I formed relationships with my kids.

My first year as a district leader was marked by reticence, anxiety, and self-doubt. Without the necessary experience to effect positive change early on, I had to retreat to what I knew: people. I applied the same principles to leadership that I did to teaching. I invested in relationships, and I offered to help in ways that made sense for teachers, not for me. I identified a tribe, a group of like-minded Edu-leaders, and did my best to empower them on the way to their own level up opportunities.

My first year as a principal is, well, still my first year. I started the book and blog as Chief Academic Officer, but I signed the book contract as a K-5 principal. In effect, I had literally leveled up while I was crafting an analogy about doing just that. In the time since, my leadership journey has been as exhilarating and frustrating as Mario's journey. The exhilaration has come as a result of working with a gifted staff, supportive community, and amazing kids. The frustration has come as a result of my own perpetual desire to do more and to be more. Leveling up, for me, has come slowly and humbly. It's come as a result of asking more questions than I can count, of relying on people I trust, both in person and online, and of reflecting tirelessly on my practice.

Because the educational landscape is paradoxically both undulating and painfully static, sometimes we need to analogize our work in order for it to make sense. We can hang posters of cats hanging from tree limbs (*Hang in there!*) or of Horace Mann quotations from our office walls, we can read about leadership quadrants and tendencies, we can follow leadership blogs and participate in leadership Twitter chats, and we can lead without doing any of the above.

We need to level up.

Fortunately for educational leaders, our available mushrooms and flowers have increased exponentially over the last several years. Whether in response to a growing anti-education national fervor, to the absurdity of standardized testing, or to the archaic teacher preparation programs touted by some colleges and universities, educators began to look within to effect change. "Leveling up" used to mean earning an advanced degree or receiving recognition as the mastermind behind increased test scores and college enrollments. Now, "leveling up" takes the form of hashtags, Edu publications, blogs, and Voxer ("Voxer"") groups. Level Up educators go out of our way to lift each other up, to celebrate each other's contributions and careers, and to seek advice from each other. Most impressive is that we often do all of this without ever having met in person.

And still, like Mario, we all start at level 1-1. We sign our first contract, take a tour of our school, attend new teacher orientation, set up our room, panic about what's about to happen, and then we get to work. As newly-minted leaders, we do our best to feign composure and panache, we avail ourselves of the red tape in which we'll be immersed, we research ways to connect with kids and staff, we set up schedules and duties, we send out welcome letters, and then we get to work.

While we might be able to learn from the early part of Mario's journey, his is static, programmed, predictable. As teachers and leaders, our journey is antithetical to Mario's in that ours is variable, dependent, and chaotic, which is why it's imperative that we seek out and employ as many level-up opportunities as possible.

LEVEL UP LOCKER

As you begin your level 1-1 journey, do more listening than speaking. Seek out veterans and newbies alike and ask them to help you make sense of the terrain. Allow them to guide you away from the implicit negativity and apathy that exists in pockets at any school. Listening, absorbing, and digesting allows you to approach your role mindfully.

In time, you'll find level up opportunities through the connections you make with your kids and your colleagues. When you make such connections, remember how they started, where you "found" them. At some point, teachers and leaders will rely on you to help them level up. After all, we are in the business of paying it forward.

The fire flower is a mighty tool for Mario. It gives him strength and confidence. Develop your own fire flower and then share it with colleagues. Write about it. Present on it. Tweet about it. In time, it will become with what you're associated when people think of you.

There will be times, though they might be brief, during which you will feel invincible. You'll have crushed a lesson you tried for the first time, you'll illustrate to staff that the PD you develop is relevant and applicable, you'll speak to a parent who desperately needed to hear something positive about her son. Fleeting, maybe, but your stars will sustain you throughout your career.

Extra life mushrooms are rare but crucial. When you make a mistake, own it and earn yourself another life. When work-life balance pulls at you, separate and relax to earn an extra life. When you have to choose between taking your kids to the park or finishing up that paperwork, choose the former always and earn a new life.

GENRES

As video game storylines, graphics, and gameplay became more sophisticated, so too did the genres in which they existed. Iconic staples of the industry like *Asteroids* ("Asteroids") and *Space Invaders* ("Space Invaders") have a rightful place in the canon of video game lore by virtue of being the first of their kind, but gaming has evolved rapidly since those early days when there weren't enough titles to warrant specific genres. Now, without exaggeration, there are no fewer than ten gaming genres, each with a host of subgenres to their credit. As a result, gamers are drawn to genres that fit their personalities rather than forcing their personalities into certain genres.

Two genres, action, or action-adventure, and role-playing, represent the bulk of the gaming industry because of their subgenres, number of titles, and relative success in the market.

ACTION LEADERSHIP

Action, or Action-Adventure, is a common and vast genre of gameplay. Focusing on the ability to overcome physical challenges, to hone hand-eye coordination, and to overcome a series of obstacles, this genre tests the gamer's ability to make quick decisions on the way to short and long-term outcomes.

With those characteristics in mind, think about how any given day unfolds in the life of an educational leader. Without the confines typically associated with teaching (bell, lesson plans, end-of-unit exams), educational leadership is a daily, fluid series of fits and starts that can't be predicted. In this way, every day is an action-adventure game for leaders, but that doesn't mean we approach each day ill-equipped to handle that which presents itself.

Action leadership requires just that: action. Consider how often we get bogged down with the bureaucratic parts of our jobs and how that affects our ability to be active. Of course, being active means accepting the random series of events that awaits us once we commit to leaving our offices. It demands, then, the requisite coordination, reaction, and split-second decision-making associated with our action-adventure leadership.

Picture this. You commit to leaving the red tape tucked away on your "to-do" table so you can walk through your building for the next hour. You've set your away message, your phone is on "do not disturb," and your cell is set to vibrate. Your action-adventure game is about to begin.

Making a right out your door, you give a fist pound to two basketball players who had a big win last night. Another twenty paces down the hall and the Family and Consumer Science teacher stops you to remind you that the cake decorating contest is tomorrow and you agreed to judge. You stop in the Graphic Arts teacher's room and watch the kids develop album covers for their favorite artists. The teacher thanks you for stopping in.

Heading up the stairs, you notice two posters, which once were attached to the wall, are now on the floor, so you scoop them up and continue your adventure. You stop in a second room. This time it's a Public Speaking elective in its first semester of existence. The record scratches when you walk in, but you insist the student speaker continues despite your presence. She finishes and you stay for two more TED Talk-style presentations (TED: Ideas Worth Spreading). The kids did an amazing job, and you praise them and their teacher, who is beaming on the other side of the room. That felt good.

Back out in the hallway, you are approached by the union president who avails you of the possibility of a grievance on behalf of the association. He requests a meeting with the interested parties as soon as possible. You ask him to schedule it with your secretary.

Further down the second-floor hall now, two older students turn a corner, but not before one drops an F-bomb prior to seeing you. There are rules about such conduct, but you decide to pull the two kids aside to talk about what happened. One kid is only guilty-by-association, so he listens compliantly, knowing he isn't in trouble. The offender listens to your speech about representing our school and community and about the effects of foul language on school culture. He nods, but you're pretty sure he didn't listen to a word you said.

You make a right and stop in on another elective course. When you open the door, you see a substitute at the teacher's desk and think *"again?"* You make a mental note to talk to the teacher about the importance of being at work so our kids have some stability and consistency.

Heading up the next flight of stairs, you hear muffled sobbing. Two kids, a boy and a girl, are huddled at the top of the steps, the boy consoling the girl. When you ask what's wrong, neither answers, but the boy shakes his head imperceptibly, so you offer to walk them down to the guidance office, on the first floor.

After you drop them off, you head back up to the third floor, only to be stopped on the landing by one of the leads in the play who asks if you're coming to opening night tonight. You are scheduled to chaperone the play tomorrow night, so you tell her you'll be there, but not tonight. She walks away with ambivalence, and you realize you made it sound like you're only going to the play because you have to.

On the third floor now, you stop in to see a first-year math teacher. Unaware of her personal schedule, you walk in on her lowest-performing and worst-behaved class. She looks stunned, as first-year teachers so often do, and continues her lesson on order of operations. You notice several kids are off-task and that the teacher has her back to the class too often as she works at the whiteboard. You make another mental note to talk to her about what you saw. Later, you leave her a sticky note in her mailbox: *I'm proud of how hard you're working. I'm here to help.*

Back out in the hallway, you head down to the Social Studies wing and stop into a veteran teacher's class. Students are discussing the Preamble to the Constitution as it applies to our modern society. The teacher welcomes you and asks if you want to join a group. You take a seat with the nearest group, and the teacher announces that each group must come up with one addition to the Preamble and will be responsible for presenting and defending that addition. Instinctively, kids look at you to start the bidding, but you don't say anything, choosing to allow the kids to run the show. Your group decides that the document is unalterable because it still applies today. It is, they decide, a flawless document. When your group presents, a charismatic junior defends the group's decision by highlighting the six elements that make up the Preamble as they apply today. The teacher praises the group, as do you, and moves on.

Ready to head back to your office, you make your way toward the stairs. Your walkie goes off alerting you to the fact that your interview is here. Realizing your walkthrough is over, you look at your phone. You've been out of your office for 29 minutes.

Action-adventure leadership can be equal parts exhilarating and exhausting. Consider, too, that the fundamental difference between action-adventure gaming and action-adventure leadership is that when we decide to turn off the game and play again later the world we enter will be exactly the same as when we left it. Having already been in that world, however, should allow us to make adjustments to how we approach it. We can predict the pitfalls, we know when time is running out, and we know where the level ups are. There's comfort in that knowledge.

In our action-adventure leadership world, nothing is ever the same. In fact, if we aspired to or forced uniformity, we'd lose our game, perhaps without even knowing it. Should we commit to another walkthrough tomorrow, there is no way to predict what will unfold. Sure, we can apply what we know and what we've experienced to that walkthrough, but the landscape will never be the same two days in a row. There's anxiety implicit to that knowledge.

And yet we choose to keep pushing Start Game.

ROLE-PLAYING LEADERSHIP

Of course, all gamers are not created equal, nor are all leaders. Some prefer the complexity of role-playing games (RPG) to the spontaneous nature of action-adventure. Typically, these games feature a cast of characters, over whom the player has control at various points in the gameplay, each with a particular skill. In isolation, these skills help the gamer maneuver through battles or solve puzzles. When combined, these skills help the gamer traverse the often open-world landscape on the way to completing the game. Another ancillary, but important, facet of RPGs is the accumulation of experience points. Earned through defeating enemies or making quality decisions, experience points allow the characters to level up on the way to greater responsibility, more powerful weapons or magic, and a better chance to succeed.

Sound familiar?

As leaders, we are constantly asked to assume any number of roles throughout a given day.

> **Gamer's Journal:** Father, husband, leader, manager, confidant, principal, coach, spokesperson, organizer, disciplinarian, ambassador, observer, evaluator, mentor, surrogate, friend, son, brother, nephew, grandson, outfielder, pitcher, gamer, writer, Imposter Syndrome sufferer.
>
> Our roles aren't badges of honor we shine and show off to passers-by. We accept them, shed them, cultivate them, and share them because this is the life we chose.

Moreover, like in RPG games, those roles can change abruptly and without warning, so we must be mindful of what role we're playing in the moment. A misstep could cost us those valuable experience points we need to level up our leadership. However, if we approach every leadership opportunity with the understanding that we might have to adjust our role, then leveling up becomes a matter of course.

When I was in the classroom, I asked my seniors to consider all the roles they play in a given day. I told them to list everything that might apply, even if some of the roles were abstract like "confidant." Then, after their lists were complete, I asked them to cross off one that they didn't necessarily identify with as often as others. Thoughtfully, kids participated. But then I asked them to do it again. And again. And again. Until they were left with a single role with which they most identified. Watching them struggle, often vocally, to cross roles off their lists under the premise that it was "too hard" or "not fair" was precisely the reaction I was hoping to get. Ultimately, every student had a single role left on his or her paper, a role with which he or she most strongly identified. Now, I didn't ask all my students to present their final role because I didn't want anyone to be embarrassed by how they identified themselves, but some kids were all too ready to announce their "winning" roles.

After a brief discussion about the process they underwent to cross off so many roles, I asked what I thought was the most difficult question, "What does your paper look like with only one role left?"

Messy. Chaotic. Black and White. Final.

Now, consider that activity in relation to your role as a teacher or leader. What was left at the end?

Unlike that activity, role-playing leadership isn't as much a choice as it is a job description. In fact, if we look back at the walkthrough scenario, we played at least ten different roles during our action-adventure game: administrator, instructional leader, fan, custodian, disciplinarian, to name a few. On its surface, each interaction we had and each decision we made might seem mundane within the scope of educational leadership. However, each helped to develop our leadership experience points, adding to a perpetually growing cache of experiences from which we learn and grow. Moreover, consider how ineffective, how robotic, how cold we would be if we approached every scenario in *the exact same way.*

Like skilled RPG gamers, we know that, more often than not, we will make mistakes, we will get lost, and we will have to start over. The difference between leaders who level up and those who do not is the commitment to avoid making the *same* mistakes.

Now it's your turn. Choose a day and chart it from beginning to end. Use your phone's voice memo app or text yourself every time you make a decision. Then, at the end of the day, when the kids and teachers have gone home, go to your favorite spot in the school, pop in your earbuds, listen to your favorite Spotify playlist, and record your day. Eliminate adjectives and any flowery language. Record the day as if you were putting together a walkthrough for your protege to use on her first day. Just the facts. When you're finished, save your document and close up shop. You'll want to return to this later.

Rather than returning to the walkthrough immediately, give yourself some distance from that day. With its events still fresh in your mind, reading about the day won't be as powerful. When you're ready, pull up the document and reflect on all the roles you played during your action-adventure game. From the walkthrough, consider what you did particularly well, which allowed you to level up, and what mistakes you made, which helped you earn experience points.

Congratulations! You completed your first leadership video game level!

LEVEL UP LOCKER

Before you commit to playing various roles, decide what your strongest role is. Think of your leadership as a concentric circle from which all other roles resonate. In fact, talk to teachers, colleagues, and friends about how they would describe your leadership. Too often, we remain in our own headspace as we reflect on our practice instead of relying on those we trust and those we lead to help us grow. Then, determine those roles with which you're not so comfortable and aim to improve in those areas.

Revel in your action-adventure gameplay. Create or research fun ways to engage your kids and your staff in such a way that mirrors action-adventure gaming. Use culture and team building challenges in which folks "compete" for fun prizes, gift cards, or late arrival/early dismissal passes.

Ask your staff to participate in the same role activity we covered in this chapter. Though adults can be a bit more predictable by way of their outcomes, asking your team to reflect and share will produce a sense of community and camaraderie so necessary to a healthy staff.

Reserve an early year staff meeting in which you tick off all the amazing qualities of your staff and then thank them for blending all those qualities into the role of a teacher in your school. Do the same at your next administrative meeting. Do not include yourself on either list. Watch as your staff or team begins to view itself in the same way they were presented through this activity.

When you observe and evaluate staff, work into your narrative that which you have identified as their strongest role. Providing consistent and perpetual feedback with the same language will empower your staff on the way to strengthening that role and developing others.

3

CONTROLLERS

There are countless ways to track the evolution of the video game industry: the quality of graphics, storytelling, and character development, to name a few. However, the most fundamental way to understand how video games have changed with the changing times is to look to the controller. From the simplicity of the archaic Atari joystick to the complexity of today's wi-fi accessible, multi-button, multi-player PlayStation controller, gamers have seen their level of gameplay control manifest itself through, quite literally, the object in their hands.

Let's begin with the affectionately named joystick. With only one button attached to this small antennae-looking controller, gamers were very limited in what they could do. Able to make basic movements with the stick itself, players could then use the button to, say, fire a pixelated laser at oncoming aliens or shoot a square basketball in a game of two-on-two. Sometimes the button wasn't even necessary for gameplay as in the case of the widely credited first-ever video game, *Pong* ("Pong"). Developed by Atari ("AtariAge") in 1972, the game featured two lines, which could move up or down, engaged in a two-dimensional game of tennis. In this case, however, the lone red button was rendered useless.

As time and technology moved on, the video game controller has become a Frankenstein's Monster of sorts. Now capable of connecting gamers around the world, acting as a remote control for a Smart TV, or providing a multi-button moral compass, today's controller represents, in form and function, the meteoric advancement of technology and the power it places in our hands.

Educational leadership has followed a similar evolution. Using the same timeline as a frame of reference, the last 40+ years have seen a necessary evolution from the unilateral power of the one-button joystick to the multi-faceted, multi-purpose controller used today. Largely gone are the days of the principal or superintendent sitting in a dimly lit office making decisions for the district without so much as a peep from staff. I recently read a Tweet that asked how an *admin vs. teacher, us vs. them* mentality even came to pass, and I would argue that such a divide stems from one-button leadership. There also exists a nostalgia for a time when, because things were "simpler," folks suppose that they were better. Let's examine the evolution of the controller in an attempt to understand that which represents our own leadership.

THE JOYSTICK (ATARI 2600, 1977)

Though I can only assume the creators of the joystick, the

aforementioned one-button controller, would like a mulligan on its name, it did provide a foundation for future controllers. Essentially a moveable stick atop a black box and with a single red button affixed to the top left, the joystick gave players the ability to move in straight lines and to jump or shoot with the press of a button. So, to review, gamers had two options while using the joystick: move or execute one action with the press of a button.

Now, let's think about how joystick leaders, a dying breed indeed, operate. These leaders are utilitarian bosses who believe strongly in a formal, straight-line approach to leadership. They are practical and decisive, they are wholly aware of every state mandate and deadline, and they operate with robotic efficiency. Decisions are made in a vacuum and without much, if any, input from staff because joystick leaders see themselves as having ascended to a position in which they *are* the decision makers, so including other people in such decisions wouldn't even occur to them.

Joystick leaders complete their observations based on a very strict timeline, provide the kind of generic, baseline feedback necessary to check a box, and see teachers as employees rather than as colleagues. Because they are so practical, they see little reason to lead the person when they can lead the position. Refusing to muddy the waters with empathy and humanity, joystick leaders, like their namesake, move in a single direction, with a singular purpose, only stopping to press the red button as necessary.

Though a dying breed, we would be remiss not to admit that joystick leaders have a place on leadership teams because we all need that kind of colleague who can keep us in compliance and out of court. However, such leaders should not be operating at the top of any hierarchy.

Our profession and our society have moved so starkly in the opposite direction that such leaders are staring down the barrel of their own irrelevance and retirement or are hanging on for dear life as their staff does the real work.

THE TWO-BUTTON CONTROLLER (ORIGINAL NINTENDO ENTERTAINMENT SYSTEM, 1985)

When Nintendo made its triumphant debut in 1985, several gaming incarnations had come and gone. ColecoVision ("ColecoVision"), IntelliVision ("Intellivision"), and the Commodore 64 ("Commodore 64") had all, briefly, capitalized on Atari's success by creating their own gaming systems in its likeness. In fact, Atari itself had released its second version in 1982, and another in 1986, but by then the world had moved on to Nintendo as its primary gaming source.

What's interesting about the controller, however, is that it really wasn't that far removed from the Atari joystick. While it is certainly sleeker, smaller, and lighter, the only main difference is that Nintendo's controller boasted a second button, also red, for gamers to use. Gone was the upright stick for movement, and in its place was a small directional pad, to be used by the player's left hand, and two buttons: an A and a B.

Depending on the game, the function of each button changed. In some games, A allows a character to jump with a single press or to run faster than usual by pressing and holding the button. In other games, the B button acts as the "action" button, allowing players to shoot, punch, kick, or pick up objects. As gameplay became more sophisticated, one button would allow you to interact with other characters on the screen through dialogue bubbles or short cutaway scenes. While it may not seem like a game-changing advancement, imagine being a gamer with so many more options at your disposal. The thing is the controller didn't really change all that much; the game did.

As is the case with any evolution, educational leadership was introduced to this newfangled controller slowly. While many leaders still prefer single-button approach to leadership, Nintendo controller leaders recognize that when faced with decision making, of any scale, having two options, an A and a B button, affords them just that: options. Rather than an automatic, unilateral response to leadership, Nintendo controllers understand that in order to be as effective as possible, they need to approach leadership with a bit more self-awareness, a bit more reflection than their Atari predecessors. They are able to consider if-then scenarios, represented literally and figuratively by the A and B buttons. Sometimes the buttons represent input sought of other leaders. Other times the buttons represent a "lesser of two evils" decision. Still other times, the buttons may remain unpushed in favor of another strategy, one that only involves the directional keypad.

THE EIGHT-BUTTON CONTROLLER (ORIGINAL PLAYSTATION, 1995)

The ten years in between the release of the original Nintendo Entertainment System ("Nintendo Entertainment System") and the original PlayStation console ("PlayStation Console") saw its share of various gaming system incarnations and controllers, most notably Sega Genesis ("Sega Genesis") and Super Nintendo ("Super Nintendo Entertainment System"), each with six-button controllers. The advent of PlayStation, however, ushered in a new, more complex gaming controller, to match the complexity of the games themselves. Now, gamers had eight options at their fingertips and with a design that demanded that gamers be more flexible to reach the various buttons, and more precise to avoid pushing the wrong button. Gone were the days of the A/B button options. PlayStation provided gamers with four button options, a triangle, a circle, an X, and a square, available at their right hand. Further button options rested on the top of the controller, labeled L1/L2 and R1/R2 to correspond to the hand gamers would use to access them, and though they may have been used far less frequently than their four brethren on the face of the controller, each could come in handy depending on the gameplay.

As with any evolution, two reactions are bound to take place. The first is a curious combination of nostalgia and envy. On one hand, folks tend to pine for the "good ol' days" when life was one-button simpler and leadership was a title, not a way of life. On the other, there exists often underlying envy over the energetic, progressive approach the new school brings. The former is relatively harmless in that it takes on an airy, "remember when" personality. The latter, however, can be downright dangerous if that envy manifests itself in attempts to undermine the new crop of leaders.

The second reaction to a shiny, new, eight-button controller is sheer excitement over the possibilities with which it comes. When presented with so many leadership options, PlayStation leaders assume a "choose-your-own-adventure" style whereby pressing any one of the eight buttons can lead to countless, often disparate results. Witness, too, how such leadership disavows and disallows for top-down, "my way or the highway" leadership because the highway has seven other off-ramps.

PlayStation leaders, be it by nature or by nurture, welcome possibility. In fact, they may even be consumed with it. Such leaders are able to build teams with varying and complementary strengths, to see themselves as instructional leaders, researchers, and managers, to approach the myriad complexities of the position with their fingers on eight buttons, rather than on just one.

The video game industry (and its corresponding controllers) is now in its eighth generation in just under fifty years. As such, the speed at which gaming evolves will constantly be in competition with itself. By way of contrast, educational leadership and school reform are moving at a pace best described as glacial. Believe it or not, Atari joystick leaders are still sitting in offices around the country, refusing to admit their time has come and gone; Nintendo leaders are still in a unique position to scoff at their Atari forefathers while refusing to join PlayStation leaders on their crazy, eight-button journey; and PlayStation leaders are finding new and innovative ways to lead our profession forward despite the multifaceted way in which they view their own leadership.

Gamer's Journal: There are days in leadership, and then there are days in leadership. During my first couple months as a principal, I joked about seeing how long I could extend the honeymoon phase. Because of my talented and closely-knit staff, my transition to principal from a district position was relatively smooth. While I had my share of days that went by in a blur simply by virtue of the volume of things I had to do, it wasn't until November 2nd, 2018 (Day 90 of my game) that I had to push a series of buttons, in a very precise order, on my own controller.

It went something like this (in order): head lice, emotional parent meeting after helping her often late, anxiety-riddled son get to class, parent complaint that demanded police intervention, instructional assistant interview, meeting with superintendent to discuss steps I needed to take about police matter, canceled post observation, impromptu lunch with a troubled kindergartner whose step dad forgot to pick him up, quick game of football at recess, return to police matter, kindergartner who brought a cell phone for "emergencies" and then was showing a friend videos, finalize police matter, 504 meeting.

Decisions came in waves, buttons had to be pushed, and sometimes pushed again, and it will go down as my trial-by-fire level up day. I survived. You will, too.

Whether we are more comfortable with one-button leadership or with eight button leadership, we will still have to push some combination of buttons daily. Sometimes pushing those buttons might get us closer to our princess; sometimes pushing those buttons might make us less powerful. In the end, we are the ones holding the controller.

LEVEL UP LOCKER

With which controller do you most identify? Is your leadership a hybrid of controllers, or do you prefer the consistency of the same controller? Better still, are you in the process of creating your own controller, one that is specific to your style and from which other leaders can learn?

Reflect on a time when you pushed the right buttons and how that felt. Now do the same for a time when you pushed the wrong buttons. Again, in either scenario, the constant is you.

Consider the various controllers for or with whom you have worked. In what ways did you learn from such leadership?

Perhaps it's best to think of the controllers in the context of how and why we would use them. In some cases, the unilateral Atari controller can do things the eight-button controller cannot, and that's okay. As you build your staff and your teams, it's imperative that you don't have too many of the same kind of controllers. Choose wisely.

As you identify teacher leaders in your building and district, consider them through the controller lens. Release responsibility to those leaders in such a way that folks want to be led by such controllers.

4

HEROES

Every game needs a hero, and if video games have taught us anything about what a hero is supposed to look like, it's that they're not *supposed* to look like anything. Depending on your gaming frame of reference, heroes take different forms. From the immediately recognizable, Mario or Pac Man, to the more niche, John Marston ("John Marston") or Leon Kennedy ("Leon Scott Kennedy"), game developers take great pains to establish the hero's identity, provide a backstory, and create an emotional bond with the gamer. While some gamers can play without feeling a sense of empathy toward a well-crafted hero, it is far more likely that we are drawn to those games in which the hero is emblematic of that in which we believe or his mission reminds us, even tangentially, of our own lives.

Gamer's Journal: Sue Anderson, Lisa Painter, Beth Canzanese, John Skrabonja, Herb Holroyd, Gregg Francis, Casey Clements, Timothy Viator, James Haba, Anna Muessig, Jeanette Finkbiner, Sue McKenna, Dan Whalen, Dylan Fenton, Dave Walsh, Jen McPartland, Winsor Yamamoto, Beth Whitehouse, Tom Santo, Scott Oswald, Rich Czyz, Sarah Thomas, Mandy Froehlich.

These are my Edu-heroes. Identify yours by name, tell them, and thank them.

Surely there is no more household name in the world of gaming than Mario. We've used him and his mission to save Princess Toadstool several times to analogize our role as educational leaders, and though there are seemingly endless iterations of Mario's adventures, the original Super Mario Brothers version is the one to which we most often refer. Representative of an average Joe, Mario is a slightly overweight, cartoonishly Italian plumber who is thrust into a world of chaos. Not unlike in *Alice in Wonderland* (Carroll), Mario has to navigate his way through a series of dreamlike worlds in which mutated animals, lava-filled dungeons, and time-and-space bending pipes all stand in his way. Still, he perseveres in the name of love and saves the princess.

The brilliance of Mario's heroism is its simplicity. Without ulterior motives or ego-driven decision making, Mario moves, literally and figuratively, in a straight line as he attempts to reunite with his love. Nothing is too frightening, too far-fetched. He will not consider turning around and going home, and even if he wanted to, the game itself wouldn't let him return from whence he came. Conflicted or willing, it has been fated that Mario is a hero.

As gaming evolves, so do the heroes. They come in all shapes, sizes, and ethnicities. They bring with them a unique backstory from which their motivation is typically drawn. Their skills are varied, and their weaknesses are often obvious even to the untrained eye. Some are typecast as attractive, muscular, and witty. Some are antithetical to hero tropes; they are misunderstood, conflicted, or reformed villains. Ultimately, because we assume control of the game, the hero is always us.

Despite such progressive advancements, however, gaming heroes tend to be disproportionately represented by men.

In their 2007 study, Miller and Summers concluded that "Of the 49 games included in [their] analysis, 282 male humans and 53 female human characters appeared, indicating 1 female for every 5.3 male characters" (737). Moreover, "males were heroes 58.1% of the time, significantly more than females (34.6%)" (738).

By way of contrast, female gaming characters tended to take on stereotypically submissive, ancillary, and sexualized roles. They were often cast to provide the male hero with a purpose, to play the damsel in distress, or to act as the male hero's foil, someone to keep the hero grounded and to reflect just how heroic he is (738-739).

But hope is not lost. While gaming, like our society, has a long way to go to shed traditional gender roles and to provide gender equity, the industry is at least *aware of* its inequity. Without question, women are playing more, working more, and affecting more in the gaming industry than ever before (Zorrilla). Before there can be a movement, however, there must be a progenitor, a woman to whom gamers can aspire.

Let's give Mario a break as we examine gaming's matriarch.

LARA CROFT, TOMB RAIDER SERIES

Forgetting her overt sexualization, Lara Croft ushered in a new brand of heroism when she arrived on the scene in 1996. Witty, bold, and so very British, Lara has gone through several iterations since her coming out party, but her place in gaming lore remained constant. One of few gaming heroes to make the transition to the silver screen, most famously played by Angelina Jolie, she represented a new era of female heroes and, more importantly, gaming girls who identified with them.

The original Lara Croft is a thrill-seeking, treasure hunting, archaeologist in search of a lost artifact. Standing in her way is a veritable cavalcade of baddies, minions, and even a rogue dinosaur. However, her chief enemy, also a woman, is rival archaeologist, Natla, who matches Lara step for step in search of the artifact. In fact, Natla is only interested in Lara because she does the dirty work after which Natla attempts to swoop in and plunder that which Lara has earned.

Still, Lara Croft came along at a time when there were no heroines, and the market was flooded with muscle-bound, quick-witted men whose sole purpose was to save the damsel in distress. Thankfully, Lara thumbed her nose at that trope and told the boys to have a seat. She'll take it from here. Athletic, fearless, and charming, she was the original girl-power gaming icon.

Educational leadership has followed a similar trajectory. Ask a random sampling of people with what they associate principals and superintendents, and you'll undoubtedly receive responses that are distinctly masculine. In fact, a search of the word "principal" over at The Noun Project ("Noun Project") elicits 59 images associated with it. Exactly three are female.

The difference, however, between gaming and educational leadership is the latter has a disproportionate number of women already in the field, so there is no shortage of volume from which to associate with leadership. In fact, we could conduct the same survey but in reverse and ask people with what they associate their favorite teacher, especially in elementary school, and we would likely find that the answers are distinctly feminine.

According to its 2004 survey, the National Center for Education Statistics found that 76% of public school teachers and 48% of principals were women ("Schools and Staffing Survey"). If such statistics reflect opportunity and reality, why are we so quick to associate leadership with men? The answer, simply, is perception. While Lara Croft represents a gaming anomaly because she was the first of her kind, female educational leaders are common. But because of a generations-old perception of gender roles, our association with leadership, from the classroom to the

White House, is firmly ingrained in the masculine.

Some of the most powerful educational leaders with whom I've worked have been women. Like Lara Croft, they are bold, brilliant, and transcendent. And like Lara Croft, they have to simultaneously represent that which is often associated with leadership (power, authority, presence) while fending off deeply rooted perceptions of what a woman *should* be (placating, nurturing, submissive). In their 2007 study, "Race, Gender, & Leadership: Perspectives of Female Secondary Leaders," Jean-Marie and Martinez describe such a balancing act as, "a double-edged sword because once the principal is hired, she is expected to appear in charge but behave as a recognizable woman" (44).

Yikes. In a world that is increasingly fluid and amorphous, women in leadership are expected to *behave as a recognizable woman*. I would argue we would be hard-pressed to find research suggesting that men are expected to "behave as recognizable men." In either case, we should be appalled by the words *behave*, in itself suggestive of rigid norms, and *recognizable*, which is presumptuous and reductive.

But it gets worse.

> A man can walk into a room and doesn't need to open his mouth to prove himself. A female sometimes has to absolutely jump through hoops and say, 'I'm just as tough and I can do just as well as any male.' The tragedy is that you have to prove yourself to be the best. In order to do that, we have to dismantle all of these perceptions of the female versus the male gender in school administration (45).

To extend the analogy, Lara Croft works almost exclusively on her own. Though we get glimpses of her training and partnering with other archaeologists throughout the game's various installments, she is quite contentedly a loner. No mentorship meetings. No happy hours. No book chats. She's fully aware of and comfortable with her desire to work alone. When she asserts herself, with an acid tongue or fully loaded shotgun, people listen. She is obsessed with success and will risk life and limb to add to her legacy and to her treasure trove. Such a transparent personality garners her as much favor as vitriol.

Welcome to the world of a female educational leader suggest Jean-Marie and Martinez.

> I still think that anytime women assert themselves, there are people who will see them as either on a power trip or they're referred to in a derogatory manner. I think that's common among other females. For example, a female leader has to be able to play to the 'choir' who's observing her for weaknesses because she's a female versus 'Oh, you're acting like you're all that.'

> That's a stereotype of a woman who's in a leadership role and be 'all that'. I don't know that men have that challenge (45).

But if Lara Croft taught us anything, it's that being a woman and being in charge shouldn't come with an asterisk. In this way, Lara Croft is not a *female* gaming hero; she's a gaming hero. Similarly, female leaders shouldn't be recognized, scrutinized, and criticized for being female because, in the end, they are, in fact, leaders.

Without the confines of social norms and long-standing biases, game designers are free to create heroes in the likeness of what they think the real world *should* be. As leaders, we live and work in that real world, so it's time we borrow from our gaming friends and recognize, honor, and cultivate the kind of diversity and equity necessary to find heroes among us all.

LEVEL UP LOCKER

Compose a list of your heroes. In fact, compose two: one for those who represent your Eduheroes and another for those who are simply the best people you know. Then, cross-reference the lists for qualities that are similar in those people. Aspire to those qualities in everything you do. Finally, thank your heroes. Unlike their gaming counterparts, our real-life heroes deserve to know their importance in our lives.

Accept your role as someone else's hero with gratitude and responsibility. When a student confides in you, asks for a letter of recommendation, or makes clear that you have made an immeasurable difference in her life, honor that the way a hero should. When a teacher or colleague identifies you as his mentor, honor that the way a hero should. Part of heroism is that we don't often get to choose its role in the lives of others. We do, however, get to choose how we approach that role when the time comes.

Be mindful of how you interact and work with colleagues and students of each gender. Ask yourself if you give in to traditional gender norms as part of your leadership. Does gender play a role in how you discipline students? In how you hire? In how you delegate tasks? Challenge yourself to consider why the answer to these questions is often yes.

Gaming heroes understand their limitations and are aware that they need help to accomplish their mission. Whether it's through a fireball, a grappling hook, or the help of a friend, heroes possess the self-awareness necessary to accept they can't do it alone. Educational leaders are no different. In fact, those leaders who lack such awareness, who refuse to adapt and grow, are just as dangerous as any villain with whom gaming heroes do battle. Reflect constantly on your role in leadership, challenge yourself to add to your repertoire, and refuse to go it alone.

Like gaming, leadership is constantly evolving. Our world is infinitely more connected, our leadership platform is ever-expanding. Think about how many gamers get to play the role of hero every day. Whether they play as Mario, Lara, or countless other incarnations, gamers have the ability to save the day while choosing the hero with which they associate. Through the click of a button, gaming heroes are instantly accessible. So, too, are Eduheroes. Leaders around the world are sharing their ideas, successes and failures, and resources every day. Find your Eduheroes and level up.

BOSSES AND ENEMIES

Every video game hero has a nemesis — a recognizable, named, aesthetically antithetical villain bent on some nefarious plot to ruin the hero's life or the lives of those he loves. Sometimes those nemeses are just misunderstood, carnival house wacky mirror images of the hero. Sometimes they aren't human at all; rather, they take on anthropomorphic, zombified, or alien likenesses, making them even more menacing for our hero. More sophisticated villains take shape as unseen puppeteers, pulling the strings of a host of minions who do their bidding. Whatever form they take, such villains, in the video game world, are dubbed "bosses," and it's the hero's job to defeat them.

Gamer's Journal: When I think of the word boss, my mind instinctively goes to Bill Lumbergh, the slow-moving, coffee-sipping, cartoonishly unlikeable manager played brilliantly by Gary Cole in the 1999 comedy Office Space (Judge). His employees hate him, he inspires exactly nothing, and he parks his sports car in his personal spot. Ultimately, Lumbergh serves as a cautionary tale of what not to be.

For years, I've been mindful of the dichotomy between managers and leaders. There are days on which I have to summon the strength to focus on the former, but truth be told, I only vacation there. When teachers refer to me as their boss, I have a visceral reaction not unlike a mosquito bite or impending sneeze. I make sure to clarify that we all work together and that there is no working for me. Like many of us, I have worked with bosses whom I only saw during mandatory observations and at odd, accidental times, and I have worked with bosses who lead by example and from within, not from in front. It wasn't until I truly examined the difference that I was able to level up.

Not to be confused with the more common usage of the word, consider, instead, the boss as an inhibitor to growth or success. We know such bosses are present, are in our way, and are committed to distracting, misleading, or otherwise confounding our mission as leaders. As such, we know we will have to address the boss at some point in our mission, so preparation, including leveling up, is paramount.

BOWSER AND HIS KOOPALINGS

Let's return to the Mushroom Kingdom where Mario is running, jumping, and fireball-spitting his way toward Princess Toadstool. At the end of every level, of which there are eight, Mario must defeat a member of the evil Koopa, a collection of turtle-based enemies. Though each Koopa boss is relatively similar (more on that later), each holds a key to unlocking the next level. The final level is guarded by Bowser, the King of the Koopas. Additionally, Bowser has the aid of a seemingly perpetual army of underlings who, though menacing, are often more of a nuisance than they are a threat to Mario's life.

For every enemy Mario faces, he has to employ the strategy that best suits him at that moment. In many cases, Mario can either focus on defeating the enemies by jumping on them, hitting them with a fireball, simply running into them while invincible, fleeing from the enemy altogether, or, in the case of Bowser and his bosses, developing a strategy for attacking and defeating Bowser each time they meet.

Like Mario, we all have common "enemies" that attack our day. Unlike Mario, whose enemies all move in the same direction (right to left), our enemies can come from an array of directions, causing us to strategize on the fly. In order for us to level up, we have to accept each challenge as unusual, even if we've met a similar challenge in the past because no two challenges are exactly alike. Even if the boss is the same, even if we can predict its movements and strategy, and even if we do defeat it, the one variable is us. Sure, we should have learned from our last encounter, but that doesn't mean we, and the myriad factors that contribute to who we are as leaders, are the same.

By no means complete, here's a short list of the most common enemies standing in Mario's way.

GOOMBAS

The most basic enemies standing in Mario's way are the aforementioned Goombas, slow-moving mushrooms which are easily defeated by jumping on them and just as easily ignored by jumping over them. For educational leaders, Goombas present themselves every day, often multiple times a day. We have to decide if we are going to commit to an hour of lesson plan review on which we leave meaningful feedback or if we are going to get out of our offices for much-needed visits to classrooms. In either case, our day won't be dictated or deemed a waste if we don't get to those lesson plans, so they become our Goombas. We decide how to handle the necessary components of our leadership as they present themselves with the understanding that there is no one way to approach each. Educational Goombas aren't going away, so whether we squash them or avoid them another one is coming to take their place.

KOOPA TROOPAS

Only slightly more menacing than the Goombas are these marginally faster, equally omnipresent turtles. Like Goombas, Mario can choose to eliminate them or to ignore them. Unlike Goombas, Troopas require a bit more strategy if Mario does choose to eliminate them. Jumping on them only makes them cower in their shells, which still presents an obstacle for Mario, so he has to then kick them off screen. However, should there be something from which the shells can ricochet, Mario finds himself having to jump the wayward shell.

Educational Troopas are best described as "if-then" enemies. If we choose to attack a Troopa, then we still have to decide what to do with the detritus it leaves behind. If we are careless, that Troopa will come back to haunt us in short order. Of course, we could always ignore our Troopas; after all, they don't *really* present us with much resistance and jumping over them is easy enough. Once they usher themselves off-screen, we don't see them again, so perhaps it's safer and more efficient to just let them pass.

BUZZY BEETLES

These pesky enemies are equipped with a shell immune to fireballs, so despite Mario's best efforts to torch them, he will have to rely on the same strategy he employed against the Troopas: jump on them to render them motionless and then kick the shell to the curb. Again, Beetles are slow moving and easily jumped over, so choosing to attack them must come with a purpose. Maybe Mario needs to use their iron-cast shells as a shuffleboard puck to knock out a host of oncoming enemies or maybe he can use the shell to break open a grounded brick platform in which he'll find an extra life or power-up. In gameplay, Mario won't experience his first Beetle until about the midway point, so by then, he will have had the requisite experience in dealing with Goombas and Troopas to know how to approach Beetles.

As we move through our leadership careers, we will encounter countless Beetles. Again, such enemies are only as challenging as we allow them to be. Sometimes, it is easier to simply ignore a Beetle until we feel more prepared to work with him or until we have tried a number of level up strategies with other Beetles to the point at which we can assume leadership of the one in front of us. Their immunity to fireballs does present a challenge, however. Such security must have been developed over time, a biological adaptation earned through experience and clout. Beetles know they are fire retardant, so they often hang with other Beetles, presenting a unified front. Still, we have to work with Beetles every day, so disavowing their presence or influence is not an option.

KOOPA PARATROOPAS

A slightly more evolved version of Koopa Troopas, these turtles have the ability to fly, albeit their motion is closer to a bounce, in patterns that inhibit Mario's progress. They require further strategy in order for them to be put to rest. First, Mario has to time his jump so that he lands on top of them, rendering their wings useless. Reduced to regular Troopas, Mario still has to jump on them again in order to get them to cower in their shells. Avoiding them is still an option but because of their undulating movements, doing so takes a little more skill.

Educational Koopa Paratroopas, like their video game brethren, dare us to engage with them. Maybe it's the beatific smile they sport while they bounce along, maybe it's the fact that they require three steps to eliminate, maybe they simply present a challenge. Like each of the enemies that came before them, we still need to make the conscious decision to confront Koopa Paratroopas and to use whichever strategy best meets our needs at that time. While we may be able to categorize and approach our bosses and enemies similar to how Mario would, so much of educational leadership is picking those battles.

BOWSER

Interestingly, though early gamers thought they were battling Bowser at the end of each level, the first seven Bowsers are imposters. Making gamers believe they have defeated Bowser each time illustrates Bowser's psychological warfare, a wicked complement to his physical stature. The final battle, however, is with Bowser, and once Mario has defeated him, the key to Princess Toadstool's castle, and heart, is acquired. Forget for a second the physical manifestation of Bowser, and think about what he represents. Like all villains, he'll "stop at nothing" to get what he wants. In this case, it's the affection of the princess. He creates an entire world over which he is in control, he coaxes minions to do his bidding, he plays with the very fabric of time and space.

Apologists would argue that Bowser is misunderstood, beaten down from living the life of a villain for all these years with nothing to show for it. Unable to make real connections, he is forced to manipulate those around him.

It's a time-tested trope, for sure, but so, too, is the Edu Bowser. Tired, jaded, and likely envious of those around them, our Bowsers are more menacing than their cartoon counterparts because they are real — and they can cause real damage.

Don't let them.

We have too much at our disposal to give in. We have too much at stake to relent. We have too many amazing colleagues, both in person and online, from whom we can gain strength, strategy, and support. Bowsers are only successful when we allow them to be, when we give them power and purpose, when we don't make adjustments after we see what they are capable of.

LEVEL UP MISSION

Choose a day on which you will be wholly conscious of your problem-solving approach. That's not to say that you change how you would normally approach such a day; rather, it suggests an awareness on which you may not otherwise focus. From the kids throwing around a football before opening bell (goombas) to a habitually unpleasant colleague (Koopa Paratrooper), there will likely be no shortage of your own enemies with which to do battle.

Now, as you make your way through your day, consider how often, like Mario, you employed various problem-solving strategies. Were you aggressive, eliminating problems swiftly and intentionally? Were you thoughtful, taking time to measure each decision against its possible outcomes? Were you risk-seeking or risk-averse, going out of your way to combat or avoid conflict? Were you passive, letting the day come to you rather than dictating the action?

Certainly, the blanket answer to each of those could be "yes," depending on what you are reflecting, but the point is that you are reflecting. Then, as you begin to compartmentalize each of those decisions, you build your leadership capacity. Like Mario, you can start to predict when those Koopa Paratroopas are coming and with which pattern they bounce. Because you've chosen mindfulness, you already know how you'll handle that enemy. Part instinct and part muscle memory, you have leveled up on the way to becoming a stronger, more confident leader.

LEVEL UP LOCKER

Reflect on bosses you've encountered throughout your life. From that part-time job at Pizza Hut to your current role in education, you have no shortage of examples. Then, put those bosses into categories and think about how you worked with, against, or around each of them. Go a step further and consider which of those bosses does not fit into any category. Those bosses, I would argue, are the most vital. They either provide you with inspiration to create your own category or embody the kind of boss you will refuse to be. Providing context to your next educational boss will undoubtedly help you prepare for how to approach it.

Consider, too, what kind of problem solver you are. Do you typically attack problems head-on, or do you employ a more methodical approach? Are you a one-stop-shop leader, or are you willing and able to adapt to the issues with which you are confronted?

As a true test of leveling up, ask yourself what kind of boss you are. While we would love to live and work in a world in which we are always beloved and respected, we know that's not realistic. At some point in the past and at some point again in the future, we will play the role of boss. Sometimes that role is literal in that we are the principal or superintendent, and sometimes that role is figurative in that folks see us as in their way. In order to grow as a leader, it is paramount that we view ourselves through the same lens as we view others.

What happens when we simply can't strategize enough to overcome the boss with which we're confronted? For new and novice leaders, this scenario can be fraught with disaster. Refusing to adapt in favor of digging in our heels, waging constant battles against our Edu bosses is time-consuming and soul-crushing. Instead, seek counsel in an experienced leader you trust. Reach out to your virtual PLN. Start to build a cache of strategies for when those at your disposal simply don't work.

Edu bosses aren't going away and often revel in their own nefariousness. Accept both. If the current shift in the educational landscape is any indication, bosses are, if nothing else, being outnumbered by heroes. As we participate in Twitter chats and Voxer groups, bosses are harrumphing in the corner. As we lift each other up by reading and celebrating each other's work, many bosses are counting the days until retirement. As we change our schools, support our teachers, and celebrate our kids, bosses are pining for the days when "they were in school." Soon, bosses will be so anomalous that their presence will barely register on our leadership radar.

6

LOCATING LEVEL UPS

In order for Mario to level up, he has to commit to a precise and efficient approach to bonking every floating question mark and set of bricks with which he comes across. Moreover, he has to either seek out or be prepared for those times during which he might accidentally come across a level up opportunity. He has to keep moving forward, be mindful of his time, and avoid getting hit by one of Bowser's never-ending minions. When Mario is at his strongest, armed with fireballs *and* briefly invincible, it's easy, and understandable, for Mario to miss important opportunities or to become complacent, to become drunk on his own 8-bit power. In fact, when Mario is at his weakest, he is often at his most careful, his most aware. Espousing a "one false move" philosophy is a surefire way to demand precision, but it also speaks to an inability or unwillingness to take risks.

Gamer's Journal: I've been locating leveling ups my whole life; I just didn't have a name for it until recently. Teachers have always been my heroes, my mentors, and my people. My most profound memories, complete with vivid imagery and verbatim dialogue, are rooted in classrooms, around conference tables, and among people to whom I aspired. I remember a literacy lesson in third grade in which we had to come up with definitions for silly or nonsense words. Mine was "bugaboo." I remember the first time I was actually proud of a story I wrote because my teacher told me she was proud of me. I remember disappointing a favorite teacher during my junior year and vowing to never do it again because I wanted to be him when I grew up. I remember delivering a retirement speech for a man who finally helped me solve for x by giving me the confidence to do so some twenty years prior.

Each memory providing a piece of an ever-expanding level up mosaic.

Ultimately, I have never had to look very far for level ups because I have never left school.

What kind of Mario leader are you? Do you look for opportunities to level up at every turn, or do you prefer the safety and consistency of patterns, routines, and expected outcomes? While there is no question that our field has reached peak stress and there isn't a faculty lounge in America in which this isn't being discussed, we need to admit that outlets for support, opportunities to level up, have never been more varied, more available.

TWITTER

I remember the moment I finally decided to join Twitter with uncanny clarity. While walking through a frigid campus on the way to a La Salle-Butler basketball game, my friend Kevin was going on and on about how much better Twitter was than Facebook. Refusing, quite paradoxically, to join Facebook, Kevin explained that Twitter gave him access to his favorite athletes, comedians, and talking heads. He explained that he felt more in the know because his Twitter follows were discussing or announcing things about which the rest of the world was still unaware. He boasted that he knew and could "break" news to us before anyone else. While I still don't understand why he felt so empowered to share with us that a local athlete had torn his ACL, what he was doing, without question, was leveling up.

Fast forward a few years and that conversation resonates for myriad reasons.

- I now have two Twitter accounts: a professional account, from which I tweet about, like, and retweet all the amazing things happening in my district, and a personal account, from which I tweet, like, and retweet all the amazing things happening in my world.
- Through my professional account, I routinely provide my followers with district information, pictures of our students participating in activities, shout-outs to teachers who are responsible for so much positivity in our district, and links to articles and videos which I find useful.

Additionally, the advent of the hashtag, the equivalent of an online filing cabinet, allows me to invite our teachers to investigate professional development, classroom management tips, or content-specific resources. Our school-based hashtag provides a window into our building through which families can see and experience their children's day as if they were sitting next to them.

- Through my personal account, I participate in countless education and leadership chats, interact with my favorite bands and athletes, and allow my followers a more intimate glimpse of who I am when I'm not behind my educational curtain. To me, this is a crucial part of leadership. When we strip away the pretense of degrees, titles, and parking spots, we provide our staff with that which is most important: who we are.

- Frankly, I stopped watching the news in the morning because Twitter provides me all the news I need in a way that's more instantaneous and curated by my political and social leanings. Moreover, I read educational material far more than I once did because the information is so readily available. Now, because I decide whom to follow, I have access to the best and brightest minds, the most cutting-edge blogs, and a trove of leadership activities and strategies once reserved for overpriced, poorly-delivered, one-off professional development.
- Plainly, I will never go back to a personal or professional world in which Twitter is not an implicit part of my day unless a more effective app comes along. For now, leaders who refuse to join the revolution would be wise to investigate other ways to build their professional learning network.

EDUTOPIA AND BLOGGING

For decades, the running joke in education has been that we are all thieves, looking to steal great ideas from great educators and pass them off as our own. While that is one way to look at how we come up with ideas, I would prefer to consider us all selfless sharers of information. Thanks to the George Lucas Educational Foundation, sharing has never been easier through Edutopia ("Edutopia"). Using carefully curated and organized topics, Edutopia invites educators from around the world to share their experience through blog posts, which give readers access to writers as if they were colleagues teaching down the hall. Like Twitter, there is no shortage of topics to explore: from social-emotional learning, to flexible seating, to formative assessment, someone, somewhere has written a blog post about a topic in need of exploration.

Gone are the "figure-it-out" days when educators were expected to come up with solutions for problems they didn't know existed. Now, even when faced with the prospect of the unknown, teachers and leaders alike can search Edutopia for thoughtful, first-person accounts rooted in practice rather than theory. Without the often dry, pragmatic style of typical research writing, Edutopia blog posts read more like advice from a wise old uncle instead of as notes being given in a cavernous lecture hall.

Of course, reading about that which is important to us is crucial, but in order for us to level up in a way that is risky and vulnerable, we need to *write* about that which is important to us. To the uninitiated, writing a blog post might seem like something only ELA "try hard" teachers would do, but a cursory search of Edu blogs elicits countless examples of folks from all walks of educational life.

First of all, consider that writing a blog post doesn't become public until you push "publish." It does, however, become *real* the moment the idea is shared with other leaders. The latter is far more meaningful and worthy of a level up. Sharing ideas, improving instruction, and initiating change, verbally or in writing, happens first at the micro level. Leaders discuss, compare, and reflect. Level Up leaders take those discussions, strip them bare, and share them with the world.

Secondly, even if the requisite self-doubt, implicit to anyone who has written anything, acts as an inhibitor or creeps to the surface during the writing process, we have a network of support on whom we can lean for revision notes and feedback. Heck, even Mario has a brother who, oddly, is on the same mission for the same princess.

In this way, even before we consider moving the cursor over to the publish button, we have already considered sharing our ideas with someone else, which is vulnerable, we have invited someone else into our writing process, which is risky, and we have committed to a new path on which we walk with other educators who are ready to level up.

EDCAMP

Within the first five minutes of my first ever Edcamp ("Edcamp") session, I was hooked. Invited to attend by our achievement coach, we drove an hour north to Edcamp NJ in the fall of 2015. Though it was my first experience, my colleague, Dan Whalen, had already been to several and was committed to facilitating for the first time, so our drive up was a mix of nervous anticipation and good ol' fashioned adrenaline. In fact, while my first Edcamp experience was a leadership game changer, the drive to and from the site provided Dan and me time to dig into that which we believe about education and professional learning, to determine how we would work together, as administrator and coach, to best serve our staff, and to shed such titles in the interest of leveling up.

Edcamp is an unconference-style professional learning experience, often held on a Saturday, during which like-minded educators come together to learn and to share. With no formal presentations or sales pitches allowed, educators arrive at an Edcamp site for coffee and "building the board." Whether virtually or physically, a member of the Edcamp team creates a board on which folks can offer to facilitate a session, typically 45 minutes in length, which can be about anything in our field. Sometimes participants have an idea or strategy to share; sometimes presenters just want to get people in a room to generate ideas; sometimes presenters want to *try* something with the help of folks willing to help.

The beauty of Edcamp's unconference style is you never know what you're going to get when you arrive. Moreover, you might not even know you're going to facilitate until you show up, as was the case at my aforementioned first Edcamp. After attending sessions on Breakout EDU ("Breakout EDU"), which is essentially Escape the Room ("Escape the Room") in a box, and on Google Apps for Education ("G Suite"), I finished my day at a session on, you guessed it, professional development. However, the teacher who posted this session on the board was also attending his first Edcamp and mistakenly thought he would have to present, so he panicked, and never showed up.

For a brief couple of minutes, our group of about 15 people sort of stared at each other and played nice, but that was enough for me to make the most of this level up opportunity. I offered to facilitate the session and got us started by talking about an unconference-style PD day we run, inspired by Edcamp, called #talkingtech. Using the same basic tenets of Edcamp, Dan and I invited our staff, district-wide, to send us sessions they wanted to organize. From there, we built the board, assigned locations, kicked off the event, and watched as the staff learned from and with each other. So successful was the event that we hosted our own Edcamp the following year.

Since that day, my professional learning network (PLN) has ballooned in a way that has inspired me to continue looking for opportunities to level up. I've organized and presented at several Edcamp sessions, both at our own and at others, I've presented on leadership at local and national conferences, and written a book and started a blog ("Level Up Leadership") on educational leadership.

Still, I reflect on that original invitation to attend an Edcamp, on that Edu Bro car ride, and on leading a session that was seemingly doomed from the start as all part of my mission to level up. Like Mario, I had to seek out opportunities to do so, commit to them, and then see them through no matter what they may have produced.

VOXER

Perpetually behind the times on an incredible new band or hit tv show, I was way late to the Voxer ("Voxer") party. Though several friends urged me to join, I just couldn't wrap my head around using another format to seek ideas and support. What I had, I thought, was plenty...thank you very much.

By way of a simple definition, Voxer is a walkie-talkie. It allows users to speak thoughts into the world at a moment's notice and without having to stop what they're doing to type a text or email. Additionally, it connects people in a way that text-based apps cannot because it includes users' voices. There's something very compelling, even comforting, about hearing a valued colleague's voice on a Vox. Whether it's because of their faraway accent, their innate humor, or their gleeful excitement, I often close my Voxes feeling better than I did when I opened them.

Imagine the power of getting your teachers, leadership team, or even your students into a Voxer group. Professional development can, and will, happen anytime and then is stored for anyone to hear. Have a great lesson you want to gush about? Vox about it. Want to keep an amazing classroom discussion going? Vox about it. Find yourself always musing about cool leadership ideas and team building strategies? Vox about it.

The collection of folks inside Edu Voxer groups, at least in my experience, are humble, kind, and empowering. We feed off of each other's passion; we go out of our way to celebrate each other's success; we are connected to countless people whom we've never met in person, and likely never will. For a quick reference of Voxer groups across the country, check out theedsquad.org/voxer ("List of Voxer Groups").

FLIPGRID

As teachers and leaders, we are migrating away from how we were taught and how we were led. Gone are the days of hastily scribbled notes accompanied by a red letter grade at the top of the page. Gone are the days of Puritanical sit-and-get instruction, which amounted to little more than a compliance-based regurgitation of facts. Gone are the days of ego-fueled leaders who can't possibly learn from their staff because they have it all figured out.

Thank goodness.

By now, the secret is out about the power of Flipgrid ("Flipgrid"), which was recently made free for educators. Similar to Voxer in that it includes a human element to discussion and activity, Flipgrid allows users to record short videos of themselves responding to a prompt, throwing some love to a colleague, or providing students feedback on their writing. It's an amazing tool that, frankly, should be used even more.

Again, there's a palpable difference between written communication and visual/verbal communication. The former is rife with implied inflection and overanalyzed punctuation. The latter is real. It's visceral and human. Think back to your time in school, at any grade level, when your favorite teacher wrote you something so powerful, so kind that you kept it. In fact, you probably know where it is right now. Now imagine that same kindness being spoken, being recorded for you to view and keep. Go one step further and imagine showing your *own* students or children that video years later.

As a district leader, I used Flipgrid as a way for our first-year teachers to record their progress throughout the year and then to leave a message for next year's crop of newbies. We watched them to close out our new teacher orientation at the end of August. I would argue those grids confirmed for our new staff that we already knew: our district is amazing.

Like everything in life, locating level ups is a matter of choice. It's a conscious decision to reflect on who we are, to commit to perpetual improvement, and to seek out level up opportunities.

Because leadership isn't something that happens to us. We happen to leadership.

LEVEL UP LOCKER

① Think about how you've leveled up outside of education. Maybe you changed up your workout routine, maybe you started a meditation practice, or maybe you got out of that toxic relationship. If you've made positive changes in your personal life, you won't have to look too far to do the same in your professional life.

To whom do you look up in your practice? Who is constantly able to lift you up, perhaps without even knowing it, in a way that's genuine and far-reaching? Each conversation with them is impactful. Each problem you present to them is met with a solution. Each great day you have is shared with them. Those folks are your human level ups.

Create a level up "list" on Twitter. Fill that list with educators and leaders with whom you identify, by whom you are inspired. Watch, then, as you scroll through your feed and find great ideas, powerful stories of triumph, or links to a Google Drive full of ready-to-use resources.

I can't tell you how many people I talk to or who reach out on Twitter about how I decided to start blogging. So many folks have their fingers on the keyboard with a story to tell, but they just can't bring themselves to push publish. I tell them, without hesitation, that I just told myself I was going to write every morning and I was going to start on January 2. Without blogging, I wouldn't have been asked to speak at conferences, wouldn't have met my PLN, and wouldn't have written this book. I know how infomercial this sounds, but you really just have to commit to it and get to work.

Challenge yourself to create your first Flipgrid for your staff and students. Show them your face, let them hear your voice, and allow them to see you misspeak or stutter a bit. Post it to your Twitter page or school website. Come out from behind the curtain and provide people with a glimpse of who you are. Doing so will dispel any mystery, will disarm people whom you have yet to meet, and will make you a person, not a figure.

7

EASTER EGGS AND SIDE MISSIONS

Imagine being a video game developer. Limited only by your imagination, you have the power to create an entire universe replete with only that which you deem necessary, relevant, or fun. The laws of physics, space, and time only apply if you allow them to. Storytelling is brought to life through a visual and auditory representation of your vision, and you get to decide the rules. The only problem is that, upon completion, such a labor of love is then released for other people to enjoy. Sure, developers can, and should, play their own games, but when you create the map, there's little incentive to follow it.

Now, go a step further and imagine being a video game developer who wants to have a little fun of her own.

Easter eggs, the aptly named euphemism for hidden or earned rewards, are a way for developers to wink at gamers as they play. The first credited Easter egg belongs to Warren Robinett, the creator of the 1980 Atari classic, *Adventure* ("Adventure"). In it, Robinett simply added vertical-reading text that credited himself with the creation of the game (Brinks). Sometimes those Easter eggs are absurd, like a character wearing a nonsensical outfit; sometimes they are nods to themselves, like a reference to past or future titles; sometimes they are playful, like a character breaking the fourth wall and addressing the gamer directly; and sometimes they offer ways to level up, like earning unlimited extra lives. Whatever the motivation, Easter eggs challenge developers to outsmart gamers, who have become obsessed with finding such Easter eggs, and remind themselves and gamers alike that sometimes the game within the game can be just as fun.

For gamers, Easter eggs provide incentive outside high scores and defeating the game. In some ways, searching for and finding Easter eggs is akin to a dance between the gamer and the developer. Developers giggle to themselves while they bury Easter eggs deep in the bowels of their games; gamers stop at nothing to yell a virtual "gotcha" back at developers when they find those treats. And so the dance goes on.

Every game has an ultimate goal: save the princess, find the treasure, contain the zombies. When gamers press play, they've already made the decision to purchase or download that game, so, ostensibly, they also have a sense of what the game's purpose is. However, in the ever-evolving world of gaming, one goal just simply isn't enough.

Enter side missions.

Created by developers to give gamers an option to sort of push pause on the main mission in lieu of an ancillary, reward-based side mission, gamers found themselves playing a game within the game. As games began to take on more cinematic, choose-your-own-adventure style story arcs, side missions became a cooler, shinier toy for gamers. Easter eggs on steroids, if you will.

Then, as multiplayer and online gaming began to usher in a new generation of gaming, side missions, while almost exclusively optional, became the rule, not the exception. Having to rely on a team of gamers to complete the main mission is one thing, but to execute side missions together provides bragging rights that go far beyond the schoolyard in a gaming community that is constantly and globally connected. If bragging rights weren't enough, side missions also provide gamers with rewards in the form of level ups, extra weapons, or glimpses into an extension of the game's narrative. For "hardcore" gamers, finishing a game and *experiencing* a game in its totality aren't mutually exclusive.

As educational leaders, Easter eggs and side missions are more the norm than the exception. Unlike a well-designed video game in which every action has a reaction, every decision leads to a finite outcome; a day-in-the-life of education knows no script. While we can plan for and predict the events of a given day, nothing derails that meticulously laid out plan like a fire drill, child in crisis, or hallway fight. So while the overall mission of our day, month, and year doesn't change, how we get from point A to point B is in a constant state of flux. Gamers and educational leaders alike have to make the conscious decision to seek out Easter eggs or to commit to a side mission in the interest of leveling up.

MAKE YOURSELF THE EASTER BUNNY ALL YEAR

There are two ways to incorporate Easter eggs into your leadership. The first invites staff to search for announced Easter eggs throughout the year. At your first staff meeting, introduce how Easter eggs will be a part of the school's culture. Tell staff that you'll be offering level up opportunities in the form of "jeans day" passes, early out or late in passes, or free preps to those who "find" your Easter eggs. Then, create those Easter eggs in the form of challenges strategically dropped around campus:

- Take a selfie with one member from each department
- Record a Flipgrid in which you share a favorite teaching strategy
- Co-teach a lesson with a member of your department
- Host a lunch and learn in your room on a topic of your choice
- Record a student impersonating you playfully during instruction (be careful with this one)

The possibilities are endless and are bound only by your imagination. Notice, too, that the challenges should be varied in form and function. Include challenges that speak to instruction, culture, rapport, data, and just plain old fun. Then, when teachers find them, much like our gamer counterparts, they can choose to participate if they'd like. Minimally, those who find Easter eggs but choose not to play along will mention it to a friend who will.

The second, more subversive way, to incorporate Easter eggs is to make no mention of them at all. Using the same premise as the challenges above, this time watch as teachers find them without a preface. Some will think it's a silly joke perpetrated by the staff jester, some will know it came from you and scoff, still others will be excited by the prospect of being part of this secret society. In some ways, this method may provide a more authentic approach to the activity because it invites people to participate without the promise of getting anything in return. Still, through Easter eggs, you'll have created activities to offset the otherwise structured, formal atmosphere implicit to most school settings. Watch, then, as your school shifts, even slightly, toward a more collaborative and supportive culture. Teachers will begin to come up with their own Easter egg ideas, some may even suggest making a competition out of their creation and retrieval, and will build them into their classrooms. Departments and their supervisors can compete against each other, students can be included in fun ways, and all the while folks are learning and working together in ways they never had before.

SIDE MISSIONS

While Easter eggs represent the laid-back, fun extension of level up

Gamer's Journal: I miss my side missions. For most of my career, my side missions centered on athletics. Fortunate to coach baseball at my alma mater, Audubon High School, the winningest public high school program in New Jersey, I spent more time on school buses, in dugouts, and with student athletes than I did with my own family. While I coached basketball, and soccer as well, baseball has always been my passion, my ultimate side mission. Through private conversations about a player's swing, work ethic, or leadership capacity, I was leveling up. I loved shagging batting practice fly balls with our team, taking the opportunity to talk to guys about life, responsibility, and their future. Many of my current friends are former players, our relationships formed between those chalked lines, in seven-inning increments, for twelve years. Truly powerful side missions don't feel like, or serve as, extra opportunities to level up. Rather, they are woven into our lives in education, the reach of which goes far beyond the four walls of our classroom.

leadership, side missions are more akin to their more business-like alter ego. Much like in gaming, side missions are a more formal, announced approach to leveling up because they require a concerted effort, over time, to complete. Still, what we earn as a result of completing a side mission can, and should, be just as rewarding as those earned through finding Easter eggs.

Unlike their video game counterparts, however, educational side missions (and their accompanying rewards) are customized by the educator. In this way, we are in complete control of such side missions in a way we cannot be during a gaming experience. Though we control when to begin, when to pause, and when to return to the main mission like in gaming, our side missions have been sought out or created by us, not for us.

TWITTER CHATS

Over 335 million people, worldwide, are monthly active Twitter users (Aslam). The social networking giant provides a level of connectivity and community unlike the world has ever seen, and its ever-evolving platform and perpetual growth promise to broaden an already enormous concentric circle. Because users can curate their own virtual Rolodex of follows and followers, Twitter has made professional learning and networking easier, more accessible, and for level up leaders, an expectation.

Education-based Twitter chats happen daily and are designed to get as many like-minded educators in the same space to discuss what they're doing, with what they're struggling, and in what ways they can support each other. The antithesis to the traditional sit-and-get staff meeting, Twitter chats are fast moving, inquiry-based, and often celebratory discussions around a central theme: leadership, professional development, or a particular book, to name a few.

There are two Twitter chat side missions available to educators. The first is to simply take part in one, even if you don't participate (lurking, in Twitter parlance). Using a simple hashtag search, you will find an upcoming chat or an archived chat based on that search. For instance, let's say you're a new administrator who just wants to absorb the collective wisdom of veteran administrators during their #levelupleadership chat. Again, you can use that hashtag and see what's already been discussed in previous chats, or you can plan to check out their next chat and participate.

Once you become comfortable with the expectations, pace, and norms of a Twitter chat, it's time to level up and moderate or guest moderate a chat. Folks who create Twitter chats around the world are not only desirous of but also thankful for the chance to hand control of a chat over to someone who can provide a fresh take, a new voice, and a night off for its hosts. However, unlike in the previous example during which you're a more passive participant, choosing to moderate a chat is a lot of work. Among the items on a laundry list of possible expectations include submitting your questions to the chat's host ahead of time for approval, pre-loading both your questions and your own answers to those questions using Tweetdeck ("Tweetdeck"), a site which allows you to plan and send tweets at a predetermined time, and moderating the chat in real time. Typically an hour in length, for moderators, those sixty minutes are gone in a blink.

The benefits of joining or moderating a Twitter chat are immediate and perpetual. First of all, you've leveled up your leadership simply by committing to professional growth on your own time. Second, with each chat comes an opportunity to grow your professional learning network (PLN). Whether you lurk or participate, you're bound to identify with folks in a chat based on what they tweet, so the logical next step is to follow them. In an online community laser-focused on supporting itself, that follow is most often returned and, slowly, you'll build an all-star team of educators.

Next, and this cannot be overstated, folks who participate in chats are constantly sharing their best resources, favorite blogs, or most effective strategies with the expectation that each will be considered, if not used, by other folks on the chat. We all know how skilled educators are at begging, borrowing, and stealing, so a Twitter chat allows you to build your capacity and add to your toolbox as often as you like.

HOST A BOOK CHAT

While Twitter chats represent the sleek, new sports car in the driveway, a good ol' fashioned book chat reminds us that before that new car came a safer, more reliable sedan. For every level up leader willing to moderate an online chat, there's an OG who would rather dig into a book with a collection of colleagues, over several weeks, and discuss it face-to-face. Of course, doing so increases the participants' vulnerability quotient because there's no lurking in a live book chat.

There a couple different ways to go about hosting a book chat. The first, and most direct, way is to choose a book about which you can assume people will be excited, choose the times and locations of the chats, and determine about what you'll talk during each session. For many book chat enthusiasts, having these decisions made for them increases the likelihood of their participation. With only one choice and one path to joining, many folks are more likely to talk themselves into joining than they are to talk themselves out of joining. Plus, as the moderator, choosing this route implies that you already have an awareness of your staff, its personality, and its needs. Level up leaders make decisions for and in the best interest of their staff.

The other option, a more dip-your-toe-in-the-water approach, is to research and identify a handful of titles on which staff can vote. Then, majority rules and folks who didn't select that book can choose to opt in or out. However, the advantage to offering several titles is doing so forces staff to take a look at each and decide, through their own lenses, which speaks to them. Now you've asked staff to consider their own needs and practice in a way that, regardless of their choice, is reflective rather than imposed. If the ultimate decision of the group doesn't meet the needs of folks who didn't choose that title, you've introduced them to four or five other options for them to read on their own. Cleverly, you have leveled up your staff.

Once the title has been chosen, you have to decide how and when you'll meet. Because you've put the power in the hands of staff to arrive at this point, it only follows that you would do the same by way of time and venue. For some members of the group, meeting face-to-face regularly is going to be a challenge: some are coaches or advisors, many are parents with after-school pick-up responsibilities, and most are incredibly busy. Honoring the members of the group is key to buy-in so, again, put the decision in their hands. Perhaps you arrive at a hybrid approach to the chat by which you agree to meet in person every other session and convene online in between. Maybe the group decides the best time to participate is during lunch or free periods when everyone is already in the same place at the same time. Yet another option would be to hold sessions after school only but at various venues (the library, the local coffeehouse or restaurant, a member's house) to accommodate the greatest number of people.

Ultimately, hosting a Twitter chat or book club is a win as soon as the decision is made. Without anyone keeping score or including a rubric, everyone is on a professional learning path, whether that path is a direct line or an amorphous blob. Sometimes leveling up isn't as much about the destination as it is about the path.

FLIPGRID (TAKE TWO)

Level up leaders can use Flipgrid to gather feedback on a recent initiative, to post "shout outs" to teachers on a job well done, or to create a quick-hitting, pop-up PD opportunity for those interested. In fact, the more we focus on digitizing and making virtual the educational experiences for our kids, the more we need to do the same for our teachers. Flipgrid allows the reticent public hand-raisers or the insecure writers to participate in the discussion in a way that is distinctly on their terms. Because Flipgrid forces users to go through a few steps before the video is posted, users can really take their time crafting their responses, editing them if necessary, and only pushing "submit" when they are good and ready.

Another way to use Flipgrid outside the confines of your campus is to use it with any consortium or leadership groups to which you belong. In advance of your next meeting, post a Flipgrid and invite the members of the group to respond. While you may only have a few brave takers at first, you will find that a discussion among a small group of passionate people is far more powerful than a contrived discussion among a large group of disaffected people.

How about this for a side mission? Host a Twitter chat or book club to which people post their Flipgrids only. Watch, then, as the discussion becomes more human, more personal with the inclusion of a video to which people can attach names to faces and voices rather than just words.

LEVEL UP LOCKER

Easter eggs require a focused attention to detail and an ability to recall conversations with your staff. Let's say you have a teacher whose wife recently had a baby, whose name is Abigail, and is due back from paternity leave next week. Find a keychain, trinket, or pendant with the baby's name on it and hide it somewhere obvious. When the new papa returns and finds his Easter egg, he'll start his day with a much-needed smile, and you'll have leveled up.

Survey your staff at the beginning of the year to find out nuances about each such as their favorite treat, book, or sports team. Once you've collected the responses, you have a complete list of Easter eggs, specific to each person, to which you can refer all year.

Plan an actual side mission to an Escape the Room near your building. Select teams randomly and see which team emerges first (if at all). Such a team building exercise gets you off campus and allows you to work with your staff in a fun way. Then, watch as your teachers start to create similar activities for their classes. Offer to buy a few Breakout EDU kits and allow teachers to create their own content-based games for their kids.

Create a Twitter bingo board through which you ask teachers to complete a number of tasks through the platform. You can urge them to follow some Edu heavy hitters, to post a link to a great resource or activity, or find at least three useful tools to add to their toolbox. Now, Twitter becomes less intimidating for the new users, and the tweeting veterans can help their colleagues explore.

Flip the side mission script and have your staff create one for you. Show that you're both vulnerable and reflective. This could be a great way for your staff to make suggestions about your leadership in a way that is couched in fun, not fury.

POINT OF VIEW

During the early generations of video game play, gamers controlled the hero through a third-person perspective. In our hands, we held the power to move the character through the game as an omniscient and sentient extension of the character himself. Watch gamers long enough, and you will see them move, even slightly, to the rhythm of their character. Sometimes they may lean to one side as the character navigates through a world. Other times they might try to peer around the corner of a building along with their character. But make no mistake, playing a third-person video game provides an aerial perspective necessary to save the day.

The opposite experience comes in the form of first-person gameplay. While iterations of such a perspective have been around since the 1970s, two titles released in the 1990s are credited with changing the gaming landscape simply by changing the gamer's perspective.

1992's *Wolfenstein 3D* ("Wolfenstein 3D"), widely considered the granddaddy of first-person gameplay, features an Allied spy during WWII who escapes Castle Wolfenstein and then does battle with an array of Nazis. Shortly thereafter, in 1993, *Doom* ("Doom") was released and instantly became one of the most popular first-person games in gaming history. The game's premise centers on a "space marine," a common science fiction trope, doing battle with enemies from Hell. In each, gamers can only see the action through the main character's eyes. There is no periphery, no global view of gameplay, so the aforementioned mirror movements present in third-person gaming are only amplified as gamers assume only the "eyes" of the main character.

As a result, gamers are presented with an option for gameplay perspective.

Gamer's Journal: In the five years since I've been out of the classroom, my point of view has shifted quite dramatically. For the first fifteen years of my career, mine was a myopic, laser-focused point of view, the field of vision of which was specific to my kids. No amount of PD, budget concerns, or board of education turnover mattered more than the students in C206 each year. Part naivete, part arrogance, I just didn't see much purpose in putting my energy into anything else.

Now, on the other side of the line and of my career, my point of view has zoomed out. First, my focus is on my teachers. I can't ask or expect them to grow our students if I'm not willing to support their own growth. Similarly, unlike when I was in the classroom, responsible for 20-30 students at a time, I have to consider the needs of all of our kids. All the time. So not only has my point of view changed but also it can oscillate between first person and third person at a moment's notice.

However, the most profound way in which my point of view has changed is that I am forcing myself to view my decisions through my parent lens. When I introduced myself to my kindergarten parents last summer, I assured them that, as the father of a kindergartener, all my decisions would be made with my son in mind. In other words, because my day is only just beginning when I get home from school, I consider how my son would react to a new math program, a kindness initiative, or a menu option. While he's not the arbiter of my decisions, he does give me a frame of reference, much like he did as I watched him play Super Mario Brothers. I believe that sharing that with my new parents bought me some street cred and human capital, which has served me well in year one.

Some prefer the aerial, big picture control of third-person games, while others prefer the more visceral, myopic control of first-person games.

Perhaps, then, gamers prefer the point of view through which they view their own lives. For the record, I won't play first-person games because of that very premise.

THIRD-PERSON POV LEADERSHIP

I prefer to play video games in which I can see, navigate, and, ultimately, succeed or fail within a world in full view. Because I have always viewed the world through a panoramic lens, it only follows that the relative comfort of a gaming experience should mirror such perspective. As an educational leader at the district level, I think it is imperative for me to view my leadership and decision making as broadly as possible. As such, my hope is that I can effect positive change, for children and adults, in a way that is perpetual and systemic.

Third-person leadership also tends to be more proactive, more global, and more reflective. In order for leaders to lead with this perspective, they have to constantly survey the landscape for possible pitfalls and possible level up opportunities. Ours is an if-then, choose-your-own-adventure style through which we are rarely surprised and often prepared. We analyze the terrain, determine if it is something we've seen before, reflect on how to navigate it, and make decisions we believe are in the best interests of the most people.

FIRST-PERSON POV LEADERSHIP

When *Wolfenstein* and *Doom* came along, each brought with it a novelty, which gave them instant credibility. Never before had gamers had the opportunity to assume the role, quite metaphysically, of the main character. In this way, gamers are no longer detached from the gameplay, no longer pulling the strings of their heroes from on high. Rather, first-person perspective challenges gamers in a far more nuanced way because they have to live and react exactly as they would in real life. Calling on parts of their own ego, gamers who prefer first-person perspective don't operate as part of a bigger picture because they literally can't see any further in front of them than this perspective allows. Again, for some, that prospect is exhilarating. For others, like me, that prospect is riddled with anxiety.

First-person leadership isn't better or worse, necessarily, than its third-person counterpart. In fact, my wife and I debate this constantly because, as I mentioned earlier, I live my life from a third-person perspective, and it shapes all my decision making. She, on the other hand, is staunchly in the first-person perspective camp. In fact, when we discuss this dichotomy as it pertains to our marriage and our parenting, her perspective makes more sense to me than mine does to her. Why focus on everything, she would argue, when it's difficult enough to focus on one thing at a time?

While I have tried first-person gaming, I admit that I am not just not good at it. Whether because I can't help but apply my third-person worldview to the game or because I am too busy craning my real neck to see what is around my pretend character, I just don't prefer the perspective. However, just because I don't prefer the perspective doesn't mean I can't appreciate its place in gaming or in leadership. In some ways, I envy leaders who can lead with a laser-like focus on only what's directly ahead.

Like in gaming, leadership perspective is as innate as it is visceral. During a recent interview I gave, the interviewer started by asking me if leaders are made or born. While it's not a question I hadn't heard before, especially after decades of playing and coaching sports, it was the first time it was posed to me directly. I even joked with her that she wasted no time getting to the deeply personal, psychological question. While I did pause to consider the question, ultimately, I knew the answer as soon as the question was asked.

Leaders are born, not made.

While an argument could be made to the contrary, I would argue that if a leader is made, it's only done so in the likeness of someone who was born as such. There is, then, an innate quality to leaders the origin of which we often cannot pinpoint. However, the lens through which we lead is a choice we make as we determine how we want to experience that leadership. Though both perspectives are, in fact, visceral, each owes to a separate set of rules, of expectations, and of outcomes. Third-person leaders bear the weight of the entire organization daily and make decisions knowing they will affect a great number of people for better or for worse. First-person leadership deals not with the periphery of decision making because doing so disregards the immediacy of what is directly ahead.

Not sure about from which perspective you will, or tend to, lead? Picture this.

You are tasked with developing a professional development day from 8-1 for your K-12 district. It's scheduled for February, during a contract year, and you get the sense that your teachers have just had it. They're tired. They're deflated. They're likely not going to be down with the planned PLC share out session. Still, you have things you know you need to do, and your team is looking to you to make this all work.

A first-person leader and third-person leader will undoubtedly approach this scenario differently. How would you handle it?

First-person: Stay the course. We committed to the PLC plan and schedule in August, and this time is invaluable for folks to share out their progress, gather feedback from colleagues, and prepare their next steps. We also wanted to allow the math and ELA teams to meet to examine testing data, and the special area teachers requested time to meet. Everyone is tired in the dead of winter. We'll get through it together.

Third-person: This is not good. If we try to stay the course, the teachers will resent our inflexibility, and we take a giant step back. But what about those PLCs? The data? Ugh. Ok, here's what we'll do. We'll call attention to the stress and fatigue. We'll give it a name and recognize its collective power, and then we'll do whatever we can take its power away. Let's give time back to the teachers. Let's fully decompress, as a collective unit, in a way that is fun and collaborative. We'll adjust the rest of the PD for the year to allow for the time we replaced. This is too important to let slip through our fingers.

Neither of these approaches is the *right* way. So much is dependent upon your staff and your leadership team, particularly at the top. We are besieged by mandates and protocols, which cannot be ignored. We are also in the business of people, of human connections, which cannot be ignored. Developing your leadership point of view demands an awareness of both, a delicate balancing act between the two, and an insistence that should that fulcrum topple, it does so on the side of people.

LEVEL UP LOCKER

Consider changing your point of view in micro ways. Reorient the design of your office, move a bookshelf to the hallway for kids to see, change the lighting. Each can wipe off the smudges on the lens through which you currently see the world and your role in it.

Like I mentioned in the chapter, talk to your spouse, partner, or close friend about how you each view the world. Your points of view, whether they align or are disparate, can help shape how you lead.

A vital part of point of view is considering how your staff views its role in your school or district. The only way to find out is to ask.

Then, ask the kids. Ask them informally, ask them in an assembly, create a Google doc. Determining your kids' point of view will help you and your staff develop strategies, activities, reading selections, and service projects that will shape your culture.

Want a real challenge? Hop online and try a game like Minecraft ("Minecraft"). In fact, hop online and watch a game of Minecraft. Because the game offers both first-person and third-person options, you can get a feel for both. Without question, your sensibilities will be drawn to one or the other. Then, apply the comfort, or discomfort, to your own leadership, and you'll have leveled up through point of view.

9

WALKTHROUGHS

Sometimes we just need someone to tell us what to do.

Before the rise of live streaming and YouTube, gamers who found themselves stuck at a particular part of a game, unable to solve a perplexing puzzle or to defeat a menacing boss, turned to a text-based walkthrough for a step-by-step breakdown of what to do. Furthermore, quality walkthroughs included everything from locations of power-ups and Easter eggs to detailed backstories of the game's characters.

Gamers create walkthroughs so their gaming brethren can experience the same exhilaration of successfully navigating a game without all that pesky trial and error to get in the way. Then, those creators build a bit of a fanbase of their own as gamers recognize and appreciate the creator's expertise.

Remember, the gaming community is tightly-knit, and while competitive by nature, a hierarchy exists largely based on the haves and the have-nots: gamers who create walkthroughs and gamers who use walkthroughs. Still, the collective mission of the gaming community is to beat the game or the opponent and to earn the top score. There are no gaming bylaws that dictate those need to happen uniformly. In fact, the beauty of gaming is in the symbiotic nature of its process: part autonomy and part collaboration.

Of course, there is a flip side to that mindset. The gaming community is, in its own way, also very proud. In this way, the thought of using a walkthrough, especially based on the past success of another gamer, is blasphemy. Most gamers didn't sign up for this life so they could simply follow the blueprint of another. In fact, gaming pride is as intense as, say, athletic or dramatic pride but without the household names with which to compare. Imagine if someone told Mike Trout, one of the world's best baseball players, or Meryl Streep, one of the world's finest actors, "sure, you're amazing, but you just followed _____'s blueprint." While everything in life is derivative, passing yourself off as original while you're reading from a script someone else wrote leans more toward disingenuous than derivative.

In the end, rarely will gamers overcome that once insurmountable challenge, walkthrough or not, and be asked, "yeah, but did you use the walkthrough?" The boss has been defeated, the princess has been saved, so what difference does it make how each was accomplished? What if being so obstinate that refusing to admit you need help, refusing the walkthrough, meant you remained in a perpetual state of stall? Unable to move forward, you miss opportunities to explore other games because you deem it more important to plod through your own prideful march than to ask for help, grow, and move on.

Gamer's Journal: I remember with frightening clarity the first time I realized walkthroughs existed. In 1997, I was a junior in college and the internet was just beginning to announce its presence on campus. At the time, my game-du-jour was the original Resident Evil ("Resident Evil"), a survival horror game in which you have to investigate and stop a zombie apocalypse. Since then, the title has gone on to become one of the most popular in gaming, with dozens of incarnations and six film adaptations. But in 1997, I was in my parents' basement (cliché alert), and I was stuck. So stuck, in fact, that though I knew I was well into the game, I retraced my steps to the beginning and effectively started over. It was a colossal waste of time and a low point in my gaming career, and I was ready to bag it.

Back on campus and waiting in line for the only computer lab, I started to wonder to myself if anything was available on the still fledgling world wide web. Once inside, I entered "Resident Evil" into the Ask Jeeves web browser (you read that correctly), and voila! Not quite the Holy Grail but through utter frustration and admitted defeat, I stumbled upon walkthroughs, and I would never be the same.

In the years that followed, I became a lazy shell of my gaming self. Whenever I got stuck for more than, say, thirty seconds, I would just go to the walkthrough. I convinced myself that I didn't have the patience, time, or willpower not to, so I breezed through games quickly. Now, walkthroughs are in video form, are narrated, and are ubiquitous. Still, if it weren't for that original walkthrough, a screenshot of which appears in this chapter, my gaming career might have come to a sad, zombie-infested end.

In each chapter of *Level Up Leadership*, we try to draw parallels between gaming and leadership, but no closer line can be drawn between the two than in this chapter. Pride is so powerful because it can simultaneously propel us forward and hold us back. As you read the opening to this chapter, your mind undoubtedly provided you with images of leaders with whom you worked who would refuse the walkthrough. You know the ones I'm talking about. They haven't done anything new in years, they harrumph at the mention of Twitter, they are uber concerned with the placement of your fire drill evacuation sign, and they provide exactly nothing to inform or improve your instruction. Though they so desperately need the help of a walkthrough, these leaders refuse under the banner of their own pride, or ignorance, flying conveniently overhead during a leadership career marked by irrelevance.

Of course, your mind may have wandered in the opposite direction while reading the introduction. You think, "this reminds me so much of _____. She's always asking for help when she needs it and is always trying new things." While there is a misconception that "new things" always means "my new things," those new things often come from somewhere else, from someone else's walkthrough. Furthermore, there are no asterisks hovering ominously over the heads of teachers and leaders who try new things they learned by reading someone else's walkthrough. Actually, maybe there should be so everyone reaping the benefits of working with such a leader can see the power of vulnerability and self-awareness.

Years ago, teaching journals were all the rage. I remember sitting in undergrad courses and listening to professors suggest that we keep a daily journal. "Nothing formal," they'd say. "Just something to remember things that worked and things that didn't." At the time, our 22-year-old selves nodded and made plans to do just that. Then, a week into taking over full-time during student teaching, we were thankful just to survive. Journaling became secondary to napping, planning, and about a hundred other things. Those journals would have to be written in our minds because few of us had the time to do so with pen and paper.

Level Up Leadership
Brian Kulak

Something funny happens along the way during a career in education. A seismic shift in personality and perspective, though taking place almost imperceptibly, occurs as a result of experience. Suddenly, we look up, or back as it were, and we are twenty years into a career full of stories, full of advice, full of things we should have journaled. We curse ourselves for having not written so much of it down, for trusting a memory we knew would worsen over time. And then a chasm begins to develop between folks who mourn the passing of those twenty years by acting as if they, the world, and the profession haven't changed and those who consciously commit to reflecting on those twenty years in a way that is both cathartic and honest: they write walkthroughs.

9.1/ THE MANSION
After talking to Wesker and Jill in the main hall, go to investigate the dining room. Go to the right door to one of the end of the corridor. Something terrible is acting on your eyes. Avoid the zombie and return to the hall, Chris doesn't see Jill and Wesker. Let him collect Jill's gun and continue. If you return to the place where you first meet the zombie and shoot, check the corpse it was eating, you'll realize it's Kenneth. Get two clips from him and there are nothing to do here. Return to the main hall, go upstairs. In the right there are two doors. You should go to the deeper door and get the Small Key. If you go out, you'll see Forest Speyer's corpse. Get his clip (be careful of the crowns). Return to the 2nd floor hall and go to the left room.

Source: Resident Evil: Director's Cut - Walkthrough/FAQ
(2001)

Thanks to the recent boon of education writers and publishers, there is no shortage of walkthroughs at our disposal. Blogs and Twitter chats abound and have taken very specific shapes and sizes; there is quite literally something for everyone. Like their gaming counterparts, educators are walking us through their experience with visceral detail and naked honesty. What's more is that many are written by folks of a certain age who sat in those same undergrad classes I mentioned earlier, but now they're grownups with experiences and stories to share. We have an obligation to provide walkthroughs for the next generation of teachers and leaders, so we need to do so by reflecting on our careers in ways that may be uncomfortable, may evoke pain, may leave us open to an increasingly critical world.

Maybe you decide to start small and hop onto a Twitter chat. With relative anonymity, you can simply follow along without posting anything of your own. For instance, one of my favorite chats is #satchat, a weekly Saturday morning chat that covers an array of educational topics each week. While I may not feel compelled to post (read: I almost always do), I can still experience the hour-long chat and apply that which best meets my leadership needs. Months ago, the chat discussed digital citizenship, and leaders from all over the country were posting anecdotes, advice, and infographics in support of formalizing digital citizenship as part of the curriculum. While I didn't post anything, one tweet stuck with me:

> I hear digital "footprint" a lot, but I have shifted that to say "digital tattoo" It is much harder to remove a tatoo and try to use that reference to drive the point home to be SMART and safe online #satchat
>
> 5:15 AM - 12 May 2018

Now, this tweet was retweeted at least 74 times, which means it was seen by the collective followers of 74 folks, and liked over 225 times. In Twitter terms, this is by no means a viral tweet and won't go down in a digcit hall of fame, but it spoke to me. Moreover, Twitter introduced a new function that allows users to bookmark a tweet. So as you get comfortable navigating the vastness of Twitter, you can save tweets like this one, thereby creating your *own walkthrough* on your terms.

In time, you'll become more acclimated to the Twitterverse, more comfortable with its power, and more confident in your own voice. Then, you start to post to your favorite chat and watch as your professional learning network (PLN) begins to grow. Unlike its video game predecessors, Twitter chats provide a reciprocal relationship between walkthrough writers and their followers. Sure, we could always email our favorite video game walkthrough writer to thank her for that clever trick in *Silent Hill* ("Silent Hill"), but there wasn't an exchange of ideas; in fact, there wasn't even an exchange of pleasantries. Now, Twitter allows us to curate relationships with like-minded folks who are genuinely interested in our experiences and from whom we seek advice.

The next logical step, then, is to expand your writing to a blog. Remember those ill-fated journals we discussed at the beginning of the chapter? The premise behind the power of writing about our experiences hasn't changed, but the medium has. Instead of writing surreptitiously in a leather-bound journal for an audience of one, blogging has become a way for educators to share their collective experience with the world. Blogging, then, is the closest cousin to the original gaming walkthrough; one person's experience, for better or for worse, laid out for the world to see.

Like the walkthrough, blogging is autonomous and without conditions. Because writers are in full control of what they put on paper, they can write with confidence and openness, free from the confines of an editor or publishing house. As such, gaming walkthrough writers can spend a sentence or two describing how difficult a particular part of a game is, thereby humanizing what can often read like a how-to manual. By way of contrast, blogging is less of a how-to manual and more reflective and personal. Still, in each case, writers are announcing their experience to the world, virtual or real-life, and inviting others to experience it with them.

Before you dive headlong into the cathartic and bare-naked world of blogging, investigate and follow a handful that speak to you. Because the blogging market is currently flooded, there is no shortage of options, which means there's something for everyone. Some are a perfect companion to your morning cup of coffee, others would serve as a cool way to engage a department meeting audience, and many provide perspective we often so desperately need.

While you peruse, pay close attention to the style and format of each blog. Not all walkthroughs are created equally, and the same is true for blogs. Some are heavy on theory, others on practice; some are anecdotal; others blend in pop culture; some are content specific; others are universal. The more you immerse yourself in the world of blogging, the more comfortable you'll be writing your own.

A common refrain among aspiring bloggers is "what if no one reads it?" Like our walkthrough brethren, the fear of failure is omnipresent but misguided. Let's say I finish the latest "must-have" video game of 2018, and I'm ready to create a walkthrough of my experience.

Though laborious, I replay the game and chart my path in preparation for releasing my walkthrough into the gaming wild. Finally, I finish and am ready to push publish on the walkthrough. Once I do, the walkthrough is available for the world to see, and by proxy, so am I. The beauty of the walkthrough is in its relative anonymity. It's not like I'll be in the middle of a town hall meeting fielding questions and deflecting criticism. Rather, my work is shared with a nameless, faceless population of people who may need my help. Whether one person or a million people use my walkthrough is out of my control, so in this way, failure isn't even a possibility.

The same is true for blogging.

Like I said at the beginning of the chapter, sometimes we just need someone to tell us what to do. If you're reading *Level Up Leadership*, you're reading a walkthrough.

LEVEL UP LOCKER

1 Start with a fact-finding mission centered around the question: What are you reading right now? Your staff can respond chorally or via a Google form, and you can get a sense of what folks are reading. Then, through your own suggestions, you can make your staff aware of what you're reading, which can include impactful blogs you want them to check out.

Share some of your own writing. While this can be tricky because you want to avoid the perception of arrogance, providing a walkthrough highlights your own vulnerability. Write or choose something that speaks to a mistake you made or an awareness at which you arrived. For instance, when I first started blogging, I created a "Mistakeume," a list of leadership mistakes I made in resume form. Then, I shared that with my staff during my welcome back email. Because I was new to the position, I wanted staff to see me as human and fallible as I am. Finally, assure staff you don't expect them to do the same and share it with you, but you do believe in the power of reflection, and by showing them your own, you've practiced what you've preached.

Download and print an excerpt from an actual video game walkthrough. Keep it short and sweet. Then, budget 20 minutes during a faculty meeting or PD day to have staff mimic that walkthrough for their instruction. Maybe it's for an amazing read-aloud they just finished, maybe it's in reference to math centers, or maybe it's non-instructional and speaks to how a classroom management issue was mitigated. Even if you do it once and never again, you'll have sparked the idea of a walkthrough in the minds of your staff, and you'll have created a cache of "just-in-case" walkthroughs available to everyone.

Better yet: ask the kids to create a walkthrough of their day or of their favorite part of the day. Stress that it doesn't have to be part of their school day. Rather, you just want them to invite you into their world through a step-by-step account of that which is important to them. Then sit back and, depending on the grade level, read about pet turtles, summer camp, and first loves.

Read. Commit to at least 2-3 education-based titles a year. For some, that's a month's worth of reading, but for others, that represents the ceiling. Regardless, finding pockets of time to read others' walkthroughs is cathartic, inspirational, and necessary. Most are easy reads, with life-affirming messages easily applied to our own practice, and are rife with digestible excerpts which can be used in a myriad of ways.

🏁 10

MULTIPLAYER LEADERSHIP

As gaming norms and capabilities developed, so too did the number of players who could play simultaneously. Early iterations of multiplayer gaming included "two-player" games during which gameplay was shared between two players but not at the same time. For instance, Mario would begin his game and continue until his first "death" at which point his turn is paused, and Luigi's game would begin. While this allowed friends to play at the same time, it was a bit like standing in line at an arcade and waiting to drop your quarter in the slot.

Over time, game developers began to consider how to allow two or more players to enjoy gameplay *simultaneously* through splitting the screen into quadrants, so everyone could experience the game at the same time, through creating gameplay partnerships or competitions. Thus, gamers were responsible for the support or defeat of each other in real time; or through a limited Artificial Intelligence factor, so gaming was more authentic and cause-effect based rather than pre-determined by the computer.

With the advent of the internet, multiplayer gaming exploded in such a way that the gaming industry became just that, an *industry*, replete with international competitions, sponsored gamers, and the opportunity to list "professional gamer" as an official job title. Single-player, isolated gameplay didn't die, per se, but it became the grandfather to a generation of gamers who understand its place in gaming lore but only in a nostalgic, far-off way.

Whether for the purposes of competing with or competing against other gamers, creating a multiplayer team is paramount to the gaming experience. Like any athletic team, the individual skills of any one player has to be weighed against the overall needs of the team. Load up with too many of the same kind of player and the team is destined to fail.

Of course, there's a profound difference between creating a team and joining a team. The former is often associated with years of experience, a connection to a particular style or genre, and even some street cred that precedes you. The latter is associated more closely with inexperience, a desire to join an established group, and a particular set of skills to offer an existing team. The similarity between the two is that each can take years to develop despite their seemingly disparate descriptions.

CREATING THE TEAM

Quickly, I realized that my superintendent had all the requisite characteristics of the kind of leader I aspired to be. He is articulate, student-centered, prescient, and tireless. He is also a former high school math teacher who can seamlessly break down a budget to our board of education and community. He rarely makes mistakes.

Still, he's one person charged with the care and growth of eight buildings. His hire, some nine years before mine, came at a time when he was able to build his team, for the most part, thanks to a windfall of retirements and resignations. Now, the easy thing to do would be to go find like-minded people and fill his leadership roster with people like him. After all, at that point he had established himself as an educational leader and district manager, a rare breed indeed, so forming the district leadership team in his likeness would have caused no more than a whimper from the staff and community. But that's not what he did.

Instead, he considered the needs of the district based on two factors: (a) the best candidate (b) instructional leadership potential. While such a recipe might seem obvious, or even easy, finding the best person who can also provide the district with something it doesn't already have is challenging. It's also imperative.

In the end, he has people in every position who have separate but equal specialties. For instance, our elementary principals' backgrounds include math specialist, special education specialist, literacy specialist, former high school English teacher, former elementary teacher, and former pre-k teacher. In sum, there isn't a stone unturned in our elementary ranks because our superintendent built his team that way.

Think about what that does for our district, one to which other districts often come for ideas. When an instructional leadership question comes across his desk, though he can often answer it himself, he has a specialist to answer it. When he has surveyed the educational landscape and decided it's time to make a shift, to try something new, or to address a pressing need, he already has one or more leaders in place to run the show. When state monitors come in for review, many of us have already been working on compliance-based quality assurance, so the relative stress of such an audit is mitigated by the comfort of a functional, efficient team.

Our superintendent has often said that the single most important job of any administrator is to hire the best teachers. Without them, we are nothing more than an educational Sisyphus, having to start over again and again. The same could, and should, be said about creating an administrative team. In fact, hire all the best teachers you want, but put them with a weak leader and they are less likely to grow and more likely become complacent or leave. Neither benefits our kids.

Now, part of hiring a versatile, specialist-laden team is the superintendent's level of awareness. First, he has to look at what he has inherited and weigh that against what he brings. Too often, new leaders are hamstrung with comfortable, veteran teams who scoff at the notion of change and prefer to do things "the way they've always been done." Before a new superintendent can hire anyone, she has to decide how to approach such a fixed mindset. Because educators have protection in the form of tenure, cleaning house isn't an option — but neither is accepting that the team is the way it is and will not change. Rather, leaders who level up will find ways to best use the skills of the existing team.

Once she has chessmastered her current pieces into place, it's time to hire the rest of the team. Interestingly, finding players to fill a roster doesn't start with an outward search. On the contrary, level up leaders first must look within and accept that it is impossible to do all things well all the time. Then, the focus shifts from what the district *wants* to what the district *needs*. For instance, the superintendent may recognize that the current team is made up of several leaders of a similar background, none of which is in math. Considering that discrepancy against sluggish math scores, she sets out to find an educational leader who is, first and foremost, an instructional leader in math. While applying such filters to the search criteria does limit the pool of applicants, and doesn't guarantee that she finds someone who fills that need, *what* she wants supersedes *who* she wants. Next, she pulls resumes to fit those specifications and begins interviewing. During those interviews, she makes it clear that she is looking for someone who can become the district's math specialist. Such transparency makes clear to the applicant that her content background is as important as her leadership potential and helps to frame the district's vision for her as she moves throughout the interview.

Eventually, the team is formed and becomes aware of its collective personality.

JOINING THE TEAM

My path to multiplayer leadership was equal parts frustrating and worthwhile. A 17-month journey from the classroom to my first position as Chief Academic Officer included being a bridesmaid four times, including once in my own district. Eventually, I reached a point at which I was ready to take *any* position to end the interminable process. When I finally did get an offer, it was from the same district at which I interviewed for a different position immediately after grad school, so I had truly come full circle.

Moving from the classroom right into a district-level position was as exhilarating as it was terrifying. No amount of graduate school preparation could have prepared me for the relative vastness of my position's responsibilities. While friends were joining teams as vice-principals tasked with discipline and some instructional supervision, I was responsible for curriculum and instruction, professional development, Title II, secondary literacy, among a host of other things. But because I knew I was joining an established, highly functional, collaborative team, I never felt overwhelmed or isolated. In short, this was not a reclamation project position; rather, it was a position that would allow me to learn and grow on my terms while still moving the district forward and checking off compliance-based boxes. While I might never know if my superintendent was hiring the *what* before the *who*, as I mentioned earlier, I'd like to think that the latter gave him the confidence to rethink what he wanted from the former.

I was the newest, and second-youngest (37), member of the team. Though not under contract yet, I chose to attend the team's summer retreat because I was (a) desperate to get started and (b) curious to get a feel for the team's dynamic. Fortuitously, the person I was replacing in the position was still in district about to start his first year as an elementary principal, so I parked myself right next to him, took out my legal pad and pen, and kept my head down for most of the four-hour meeting — a meeting during which my superintendent forgot to introduce me as the "new guy," something which didn't dawn on me until hours later.

Fast-forward a little over a week, and I was ready for day one as Chief Academic Officer, a role which had changed dramatically from what it once was under my predecessor. The problem was, other than setting up my office, which in itself was a foreign concept, I really didn't know what to do. It was July 1st, the curriculum for which I was responsible wasn't due for another month, and the building was a veritable ghost town. But joining a team, any team, demands proving your worth as early and as often as possible, even if there's no one around to witness it.

Remember, joining a team comes as a result of (a) fitting the needs of the existing team and (b) advocating for yourself based on what you know you'll bring to the team. I reflected on each as I thought about how to get to work that summer. I knew my team needed a district-wide curriculum and instruction point person. I knew I billed myself as an expert in language arts and that I saw myself as someone who could serve the team as both an ambassador to the community, and as someone who would work closely with teachers. I knew the district needed a new teacher mentorship supervisor. I knew I had to start with what I knew (secondary education) and immerse myself in what I didn't (elementary and special education) in order to best serve my team.

I started by crafting a district-wide introductory email, one over which I pored for far too long, and one which few people would read in the summer. Still, that first email gave the district a glimpse into my personality and my writing style. It ended with an invitation to stop into my office that summer. Three teachers took me up on that offer, which was three more than I was expecting.

Next, I requested face-to-face meetings with each principal, at their buildings, and supervisor in the district. It was imperative that I get out of my office early, learn the geographical layout of the district, and meet with the varied and talented leadership team that I was joining. For each, I had similar questions but allowed the conversation to go where it was meant to, only offering impromptu questions as they came up. For each, particularly in our elementary schools, I led with deference, allowing each principal to guide the conversation based on his or her passion and expertise. For each, I left with a grateful handshake and a promise to do as much as I could to help make their jobs a little easier.

When I wasn't meeting our team, I was reading. And reading some more. Suddenly, the titles we were asked to read in grad school, which seemed far away and theoretical, took on new, urgent meaning. I read, and in some cases re-read, about leadership by people like Michael Fullan and James Collins. I read about literacy by heavy hitters like Lucy Calkins and Jen Serravallo. I read about professional learning communities by Richard DuFour and Robert Eaker. Because I knew the answer to many questions early in my administrative career was going to be, "I don't know, but let me find out," I wanted to at least minimize the frequency with which I had to use it.

Then, I asked each principal to provide me with a brief list of our "rock star" teachers so I could visit them as soon as possible. For me, this served two crucial purposes: it gave me a sense of what my team considered our best teachers, the endorsement of which told me as much about the principal as it did about the teachers, and it gave me a chance to introduce myself to dozens of our finest teachers, to go see them work, and to celebrate them as soon as possible.

Again, whether you're joining a team on a covert mission bent on disarming the nuclear missile in some fictitious locale or joining a team in your new district, your role on that team is as much about finding your place on it as it is about proving the team is stronger because of you.

When I finished those early informal observational rounds with our best teachers, I compiled and reviewed my notes. Through them, I wanted to come up with a common sketch of what my new district valued in instruction. I examined the similarities in lesson design and execution. Because teachers are made up of more than the content they present, I reflected on the type of person, not necessarily teacher, in front of each room. I considered what I noticed about the kids in each room, and, in the end, I had my baseline for quality instruction in my district.

But that wasn't enough.

With eight buildings over which I had responsibility, seeing our best and brightest would only provide me with one tier of instruction. If I had stopped there, my perception of our district would have been skewed, my purpose would have been stunted. Rather, I needed to make another sweeping round of informal observations during which I could see the rest of our teachers in action, but this time without principals' input. This time, I wanted to find out for myself. Each day, I blocked out the morning or the afternoon to travel to each building to observe the rest of our staff. While I certainly did not realize it at the time, committing to these instructional rounds, which were always followed with a thank you email and one positive affirmation from my visit, allowed me to level up my leadership.

But that wasn't enough either.

Seeing our teachers work and getting a sense of the district's personality was only beneficial if I shared what I saw with our leadership team. Because I was the newest member of the team, my perspective, though couched in inexperience, was fresh. Luckily, a couple of months into the year, my superintendent asked to meet

Gamer's Journal: I can't remember the last time I wasn't on a team. As a three-sport athlete, I was always playing something. In fact, even when I graduated from high school and didn't continue to play any of those three sports, I started playing a fourth. Even now, I'm in my eighth season on a 35-and-over men's baseball team, and I play eight months a year. For me, sports have always been as natural a part of my life as breathing. Similarly, regardless of the sport or level, I was always a captain, a leader, the responsibility for which I took very seriously. I reveled in being the spokesperson for our team, in being the one to tell coach that we needed a "closed door, players only" meeting, and in being the player whose work ethic coaches would use as a barometer for our team's effort. It only followed, then, that I would become a coach and that I would manage my men's team. To be clear, I didn't make a conscious effort to become a captain; I just didn't know any other way to be.

As I mentioned earlier, I am a proud alumnus of Audubon High School and its baseball program. In 1994, my senior year, I walked off the field after my final game as a state champion, the first of what would become seven for its current coach, Rich Horan. I would go on to be part of three of those as his assistant, and I keep the championship rings in my desk at school. So much of my leadership platform can be traced back to those days on the field and on the sidelines. Learning to lead the reticent, to lead with co-captains, to lead by example, to lead through failure, to lead as an assistant, and to lead through adversity all came long before I ever set foot in a classroom or building of my own.

to discuss "what I've seen and what I think so far."

Again, joining a team is rife with possibility and with obstacles. While I was prepared to present what I had seen so far, complete with copious notes and anecdotal evidence, what I said was going to be as important as *how* I said it. Make no mistake, this meeting was as much about learning about my leadership style as it was about confirming what I'm sure he already knew about his teachers. Come on too strong, and I risk alienating myself; come on too soft, and I risk losing credibility before I even earned any.

Months later, I had met with each principal several times, had seen just about every teacher in the district, and had developed meaningful relationships. Moreover, because I had spent time crafting my feedback to teachers and my observations to principals, people viewed me as an instructional leader, willing to learn from established members of the team and capable of supporting the district.

Joining a multiplayer game can be terrifying and exhilarating. Having to prove your worth, to navigate the politics and psychology of the existing team, to listen more than you speak, to defer as much as you lead all takes time, mindfulness, and humility. If you're lucky, like me, you join a team with a student-centered identity and progressive philosophy. But even if you join a team that isn't a good fit, each opportunity to lead is a positive one on which you can build your leadership platform.

LEVEL UP LOCKER

So much of teaching and leading takes place in isolation, and that's not something we can readily change. But what takes place outside the bell schedule is something over which we do have power. Create multiplayer opportunities at every turn. Consider literacy, STEAM, and wellness events throughout the year which demand that your teachers form multiplayer teams on the way to creating an amazing event for your families. Suggest or attend staff events, eat with your staff once a week, go out to dinner in the community in which you lead. Invest in your team, and they will invest in you.

Frame the multiplayer perspective in a way that makes you comfortable. Watch the offensive line protect the quarterback of your favorite football team. At the next concert you attend, focus on how the band works as one to create the song (preferably one to which you weren't desperate to sing along). Choose a powerful scene from a film with an ensemble cast like Crash (Haggis) or Ocean's Eleven (Milestone) and consider all the ways in which that team must work to create such a collaborative scene.

As I mentioned earlier, purchase a Breakout EDU kit and play a game during a PD day. You can predetermine the teams so you can watch specific folks work together, or you can randomize the team selection so you can observe who emerges as team leader. Either way, you're creating a multiplayer game, the machinations of which will tell you more about the players than will the outcome.

Examine your staff with specificity. So much of multiplayer gaming, and leadership, is identifying

the sum of parts. I challenge you to flip
that model and celebrate the parts.
Spend part of an early year faculty
meeting playing a game of "who's who."
See how much the staff really knows
each other, and at the end, circle back to
the connection they all share: kids.

Reflect on your place on your
current leadership team. Ask yourself
what role you play, what you bring to
the collective, and in what areas you
need to grow to make the team stronger.
Determine in what areas your team is
light or heavy and take steps to better
balance the team. Play the same game of
"who's who" and see how well the team
knows itself and whether it is reflective
enough to take the necessary steps to
improve.

11

WATCHING OTHERS PLAY

At the dawn of the video game boom, it was not uncommon to see several kids huddled around a single arcade game watching a friend play *Paperboy* ("Paperboy") or *Rampage* ("Rampage"). Though only one or two gamers were ultimately in control, there was something visceral and vicarious about experiencing the game alongside a friend. And nothing attracts a crowd like a crowd, so before long a single machine served as a venue, not as an attraction within that venue. Arcades were not only junior versions of social clubs, but they also became live-action museums. Instead of crowding around a piece of art that had already been created, kids crowded around each other as they attempted to beat a high score or defeat the final boss.

Arcades became communities.

As video games became more sophisticated and more mobile, arcades became less necessary. Gamers could play from the comfort of their own homes without having to use pockets full of quarters and parents didn't have to shuffle their kids off to the local mall just so they could play video games. In this way, arcades only remain as nostalgic versions of what once was, the grandfather we go to visit on holidays and birthdays. Still, the pack mentality of gamers persevered and kids began to, again, huddle around each other to watch a friend play *The Legend of Zelda* ("The Legend of Zelda") or *Resident Evil* ("Resident Evil"). Only now they did so on couches and in basements, often passing around the controller so everyone got a turn. In fact, without the blinking lights and carnival atmosphere of an arcade, the aforementioned gaming community became more intimate, more collaborative.

Fast forward further still and the more things change, the more they stay the same. The online gaming community has swelled to an unfathomable and international scale. With access to countless games on varied platforms, gamers can connect with each other worldwide to play with or against each other. While the days of the traditional arcade may be long gone, online gaming, coupled with YouTube, has breathed new life into the communal gaming experience. Now, gamers can, and often do, record themselves playing, upload their session to their YouTube channel, and watch as the views and comments pile up.

Earlier we talked about reading walkthroughs, meticulously written step-by-step instructions for defeating a game, and finding Easter eggs, as ways of leveling up. In the days before YouTube, which launched in 2005, gamers' only option for sharing their expertise with the world was to write every blessed move they made on the way to finishing a game. Even then, gaming had become so nuanced that a lockstep walkthrough was only one part of the process. Superior walkthroughs included everything from the game's storyline to its characters to its array of items and weapons, and the list goes on and on. As the person using the walkthrough, gamers had to read the instructions and transfer the information kinesthetically, which can be arduous and certainly requires a level of patience the likes of which non-gamers can't fathom.

Now, the old writing adage "show don't tell" applies to gaming in that walkthroughs are visual and, ostensibly, more accessible. Gamers can use YouTube on their phone or tablet while they are playing the game on their television. Moreover, they are *watching* an expert gamer move through a difficult level or defeat a difficult boss, oftentimes with the help of the expert's narration. So while we aren't huddled around an arcade game watching an expert rack up points in *Dig Dug* ("Dig Dug"), we are experiencing gaming vicariously, virtually, and visually.

If that weren't enough, kids, who aren't even playing the video game, are now spending hours watching other people play through YouTube channels devoted to video game voyeurism. I know this because my five-year-old son can often be found glued to his iPad as he watches other people play various incarnations of *Super Mario Brothers* or *Minecraft*. At first, I couldn't comprehend the mindlessness of watching other people play video games with no vested interest in the process or outcome.

Then, two things dawned on me.

First, this version of voyeurism isn't really that far removed from what kids one and two generations ago did. The difference, obviously, is that today's kids don't pass around a joystick or controller when it's their turn. In fact, it's always their turn because they can watch passively with no connection to the actual gamer's success or failure.

Gamer's Journal: By now, most of us have seen the viral tweet that reads something like, "One day you and your group of friends went out to play for the last time and no one knew it." I remember the jarring sensation provided by that statement's truth, and then I remember wracking my brain to figure out when that day was for my group of friends on Princeton Road. Obviously, I couldn't pinpoint it, but what that tweet did was force me to think about my time huddled around a gaming console with a group of friends. For hours. And hours.

Part of why I loved gaming so much as a kid was it brought kids together around a common purpose devoid of status, athleticism, or vanity. In fact, because gamers came in all shapes, sizes, genders, and backgrounds, we reveled in the opportunity to band together as we defended Earth from aliens, tried to win the Tecmo Bowl, or staved off an onslaught of zombies.

One memory, in particular, stands out as the preeminent example of gaming's collaborative influence in my life.

Up, Up, Down, Down, Left, Right, Left, Right, B, A, Select, Start. The Konami Code.

Chances are if you played video games as a kid, you just smiled at that last sentence. While playing Konami's *Contra* ("Contra"), gamers could enter this code prior to beginning the game and earn 30 extra lives. That Easter egg, in itself, was a game changer as cheat codes started to become more prevalent, but *Contra* was the first 2-player gaming experience I remember. Able to play simultaneously, and with the promise of 30 extra lives each, my friend Neil and I would play until our hands cramped.

But a funny thing started to happen once the rest of the neighborhood kids found out that we knew the cheat code. They all started coming to Neil's house (our neighborhood had a ton of kids) to watch us play and to play themselves. Basically an arcade of one, we passed around those controllers to watch, coach, and cheer on our friends until the waves of enemy soldiers were obliterated once and for all. Sure, we may have cheated a little, but we cheated together.

For some kids, watching another

player fail over and over again is the fun of watching online. After all, it's not their failure. They don't have to start over from the beginning or from the last checkpoint. When they're finished watching, they just exit out of YouTube, and it's on to something else.

On the other hand, maybe kids are emotionally invested and want desperately for the virtual gamer to succeed. Like watching *Breaking Bad* (Gilligan) or *Game of Thrones* (Benioff and Weiss), we owe it to ourselves to see the series through, no matter how badly we want to look away or how obsessed we become with the show's culture and nuances. We can picture kids cheering on the gamer from the other side of the YouTube channel, shouting advice or holding their breath along with the gamer. In this way, kids don't even have to buy or play the games. They can just watch and experience them from the sidelines. When you think about it, it's pretty ingenious. Imagine if relationships or careers were built in a similar fashion, like in an episode of *Black Mirror* (Brooker).

Gaming, once considered a bit of a subculture, has now become its own sovereign state, governed only by a desire to play, and to watch others play, video games.

WATCHING LEADERS LEAD

We have all heard or used the term "silo" in reference to teaching and leadership. Sure, we talk about needing time to collaborate, about grade level articulation, about vertical alignment, but in the end, we all close our doors and teach. And why not? Despite the old "strength in numbers" cliché, there's power in isolation, too. Teachers, particularly at the secondary level, are content area specialists who have both a passion for and an extended amount of training in a specific content area. As such, theirs is a chosen and preferred solitude built upon content. Moreover, content specificity acts as its own bouncer at your classroom door. After all, why would a 7th-grade science teacher want to visit the 9th-grade art teacher, right?

In leadership, silos should, ostensibly, be fairly flimsy because leaders are responsible for all those individual silos; furthermore, leaders are often hired for their ability to manage a collection of individuals, so rather than existing within each, leaders act as shepherds. Because of their unlimited access to their flock, so to speak, leaders can lead teachers to (or back to) each other when they lose their way. Professional development is created and often revised based on the leader's observations and anecdotal evidence from teachers about what the most pressing needs of the building are. Essentially, leaders are very similar to their video game brethren in this sense. They watch, over and over again, as other people "play" and determine how they can best serve those players.

Finding ways to watch other leaders lead, however, is an entirely different proposition. There are few, if any, observation opportunities for educational leaders to observe other leaders in action. It's an interesting, but entirely reasonable, conundrum in that we are constantly asking our teachers to reflect on their practice, to visit other teachers, or even schools, or to watch "best practice" clips on TeacherTube ("Teacher Tube"), but leaders aren't expected to do the same. Clearly, the barriers implicit to any leader's ability to get out of his office and spend the day with another leader are vast. But that shouldn't mean the prospect of leveling up through observation and community are impossible.

Again, as we have talked about at length in this book, Twitter has taken what was once impossible and made it possible. While participation in Twitter chats, passive perusal of an educational hashtag, or membership in a Twitter PLN aren't traditional observation, each is a way to get out of our office and observe. Because the power of a hashtag (the ever-expanding virtual filing cabinet), is perpetual, level up leaders need only to search for that which they are in need of support, that about which they have always been curious but couldn't find the time, or those in whom they can seek advice without ever leaving their office.

LEVEL UP FOLLOWS

#edutwitter: As generic as the hashtag sounds, this is an excellent landing spot for Twitter rookies. Full of practical questions, advice, feedback, and anecdotes from folks around the world, #edutwitter, and its followers, is the granddaddy of educational hashtags.

#ProDriven: Brought to you by Jarod Bormann, this hashtag is a game changer for folks looking to transform their professional development. With a weekly chat (Tuesday at 9pm/CST) hosted by a rotating all-star lineup of educators from around the country, this landing spot is engaging, informative, and practical.

The Edvocate (@advocatefored) ("The Edvocate"): An excellent edu-blog "devoted to fighting for education equity, reform, and innovation." With a particular slant toward educational technology, The Edvocate provides resources on everything from Gifted and Talented to Special Education.

The Cult of Pedagogy (@cultofpedagogy) (Gonzalez): The brainchild of Jennifer Gonzalez is among the best Edu blogs in the universe. Her writing is clever, edgy, and just what a level up leader needs.

CONFERENCES

As a classroom teacher, I would go out of my way to avoid attending a conference. We've all been to, or been made to sit through, a conference billed as necessary, cutting edge, or revolutionary only to find our minds wandering back to the classroom we left behind and the lost day of instruction. Remember, too, that as a former high school teacher, I fell squarely into the silo category about which I wrote at the beginning of the chapter. If I wasn't learning about ELA or writing, I wasn't interested.

But a funny thing happened once I joined leadership. My silo was burned to the ground, and I found myself in the educational equivalent of *Minecraft*. I could go in any direction, learn whatever I wanted (and more often needed), and create my experience as I went along.

At first, I just *attended* conferences, walking around with a bag full of quarters, waiting to drop one in the slots of workshops and sessions that sounded promising. After my first full year as a district leader, I attended *Model Schools* in Atlanta. It was at that conference that I began to see the impact a large conference has on its attendees. I took notes furiously. I shook hands and spoke with people from all over the country. I compared notes with my superintendent, whose idea it was I attend, as we considered what would work in our district. It was a watershed experience for me because it confirmed that I had a lot to learn, that there were plenty of folks like me, and that there were just as many folks willing to help.

By watching other leaders present on their various passions, I began to harness my own. Each summer after that initial conference, I committed myself to a project that would be my focus for the following year: cross-content literacy, feedback, and teacher leadership respectively. Because I had watched others espouse the power of their passion, I was able to reframe mine into separate but equal opportunities to level up and to provide our staff with the ability to do the same.

Then, in 2017, I took the next step. Instead of attending conferences and lugging around my own bag of quarters, I committed to *presenting* at them. With the confidence gained from watching so many amazing leaders, both virtually and in person, it was time to offer the same opportunity. I jumped headlong into my first speaking engagement, at the NCTE/CEL conference in Saint Louis, without so much as a guarantee that anyone would attend my session (they did) on "Building Staff Rapport Through Flash Lessons" (Kulak). At that point, I had written about flash lessons (an activity by which teachers invite me into their rooms to teach a lesson without me telling them what's coming) in Edutopia and had developed a mini following of folks who were trying it. Still, I hadn't presented on a national stage, but it was time to level up.

After that initial speaking experience, which was nothing short of exhilarating, I picked up more speaking engagements. People were now coming to watch me, and I was all too ready to invite them. None of this would have happened if I hadn't sought opportunities to watch other leaders lead.

LEVEL UP LOCKER

Investigate powerful YouTube channels hosted by educators. In precisely the same way gamers learn by watching, educators all over the world are sharing their experiences, strategies, and tricks. Start on TeacherTube.

Then, conduct the same investigation absent of education. Consider leadership podcasts, psychology case studies, or prominent social experiments to analogize your leadership.

Similarly, Ted Talks, particularly Ted-Ed, provide short, impactful bursts of innovation, creativity, and vulnerability. Watching other educators speak with such passion and conviction is bound to ignite each in their viewers.

If your district isn't already participating in something similar, shift your PD to a "by and for" model. Ditch the canned presentations by stuffy, overpriced talking heads and invest in your own people. Ask staff, through a celebration of what you know they do so well, to present. Create PD expert teams whose job it is to investigate and present on that which they have researched and are convinced will move the district forward.

Commit to a conference a year, and challenge yourself to make it a different one each year.

Then, when you're ready, begin to present at conferences. This step, I would argue, may be the most meaningful level up experience in your career.

12

CHECKPOINTS

Those early days of gaming were unforgiving. While the idea of "screen time" is a hot-button topic today, no such thought was given to the hours gamers would spend in front of their screens while playing games without a predetermined end. Gamers were really in competition with one of two things at the dawn of gaming: their personal high score or the high score posted on the leaderboard of the public arcade game. Because there was no limit to the amount of pellets Pac Man could eat or the number of times Donkey Kong could be defeated, gamers were chasing a high that was only dictated by how many quarters they brought to the arcade or how many hours they were willing to sit in front of their televisions.

Imagine, then, when the next generation of games arrived with actual missions, actual gameplay finality. Now, a payoff was introduced, which allowed gamers to say to themselves or brag to their friends that they *beat* the game. With such finality came an almost counterintuitive relationship to screen time. Certainly, the promise of beating the game would decrease the amount of time gamers would spend in front of the television because there was always an end in sight, right? In reality, finality probably had the opposite effect.

When there was no end in sight, gamers would click the power button knowing they only got as far as the high score took them and that they would eventually click the power button again only to start all over. However, when gamers realized that they could, in fact, save Princess Toadstool and that the game would end, they were likely to spend *more* time in pursuit of finality.

Gamer's Journal: I often wonder how long developers sat on the idea of checkpoints. Surely, they knew from the jump that asking gamers to finish a game in one sitting was just bananas. Maybe they just didn't feel like building in all that extra code to allow for checkpoints, maybe the technology simply wasn't available yet. In any case, the checkpoint marked the dawn of a new gaming day, providing gamers with a chance to catch their breath, go to the bathroom, or, you know, eat a meal.

My relationship with checkpoints is a bit checkered. While I remember the relief I felt when I realized that checkpoints were a thing, one checkpoint, in particular, produced the most traumatic gaming experience of my life. Buckle up.

I was 13 years old and beginning to feel myself as an expert gamer. Having defeated a number of games to that point, I had met my match in 1989's *Ironsword: Wizards and Warriors II* ("Ironsword"). The problem was I didn't own the game, so I had to invade other gamers' turf to play, which presents a host of challenges to which I was woefully naive at the time. First, the environs were not my own, so I was on a consistent road trip, perpetually the away team, each time I played. Secondly, the kid who had it, Mike, lived up the street but went to catholic school, so he wasn't even a friend as much as an acquaintance. Third, I never knew how much time I had when I went to his house; at any given moment, his mom or dad could decide it was time to shut it down and force us to play outside. Lastly, there was Tracy, Mike's older sister who will play a prominent role in this reverie in a minute.

Ironsword was a sequel, in itself a novelty in 1989, and unlike most sequels, it was far superior to its predecessor, *Wizards and Warriors* ("Wizards and Warriors"). The game was challenging, the pace was frenetic, and the music (I still remember the music) was awesome. On that summer day, I was on fire. Every move I made as the hero, Kuros, was precise. Every stroke of my sword was perfectly timed, every physics-bending jump was flawlessly executed, every level finished with equal parts grace and arrogance. But then the phone rang and my grandmother called me home for lunch. Never one to mess with Nana, I reached a checkpoint near the end of the game, wrote down the password, and pushed pause on the game, not wanting to tempt the gaming gods into playing a trick on me and erasing my progress should I power down. I headed home with a promise of returning as soon as I finished lunch.

I left the password on the floor next to the console, so I could get right back to work. Tracy had other ideas. When I got back to Mike's house, the console was turned off and the password was nowhere to be found. Searching frantically, my heart beating through my chest, I couldn't process what was happening. Eventually, Tracy emerged with a Cheshire Cat grin and a message for us, "I turned if off and threw out the paper." That was it. No explanation. No remorse. Just a sociopathic nine-word monologue before exiting stage left. Almost thirty years later, I still want to interrogate the suspect. I want to understand her motivation. But, alas, I never did get the chance, and I never did defeat the game. Scarred for life by Tracy, the evil sister who used a gaming checkpoint to provide me with a life checkpoint.

Here's the catch: despite the

promise of victory, gamers had to achieve such finality in *one sitting.*

Picture this: you've successfully navigated your way to a final battle with Bowser, and the princess is within your grasp. After so many failed attempts, you are confident that you have a plan to defeat him and end the game. You're on your last life, and there are no level ups available. One false move and it's GAME OVER. You jump, you dodge, you sprint, but, unfortunately, you die.

Please press reset. It's back to the beginning for you.

Having lived through such a scenario countless times, there is no word to express the frustration such failure brought. But, like all gamers, I eventually pushed reset and started all over again. Princess Toadstool would have to wait for me. Again.

Thankfully, as gaming continued to evolve at breakneck speed, so, too, did the plots behind the gameplay. Developers started opening up non-linear worlds full of possibilities and decisions for gamers, so, finally, games were able to be saved. In fairly quick succession, saving a game evolved from a long, text-based password to be entered at the beginning of each gaming session, to progress based save points which ensured that gamers would start at that point during their next session. A gamer's progress was never in vain.

Saving a game provided players with two invaluable things: the peace of mind that their progress was stored and a new perspective on how to play the game knowing that a well-timed save could be the difference between life and death. Between finishing and starting again.

Moreover, a further nuance was added to that precarious fulcrum between life and death: the checkpoint. Checkpoints ensured that should players reach a certain point on a given level, they would start from that point in the event they met an untimely death. Checkpoints were built into the gameplay so gamers didn't have to consciously stop and complete the machinations of saving. Again, this provided gamers with an increased level of security that their persistence was being paid off and that the chances for success were very real.

How often do we save our game or aspire to checkpoints during a typical day in leadership?

As decisions come at us in waves and unplanned crises upend otherwise well-planned to-do lists, we often look up and the day is over. And that's not to suggest that such a day was a waste or that we didn't balance all those moving parts with aplomb. Rather, leadership often mirrors those early days of gaming during which we may have obliterated waves of oncoming aliens, but they just kept coming and coming, faster and faster until we just couldn't keep up any longer.

Despite being seemingly out-of-reach, checkpoints and saves do exist during our days, and we need to commit to each in order to level up. Moreover, unlike gaming during which we are left to the whims of developers, we are in full control of how we identify checkpoints and when we decide to save our game.

KEEP YOUR CHECKPOINTS SIMPLE

Each of us endures "administrivia" during a given day. Whether it's cleaning up that overstuffed Inbox or returning that irate parent's phone call, there are things we just have to do to which none of us look forward. However, completing some of that minutiae should provide us with a brief, if fleeting, measure of relief because they represent our checkpoints. Crossing the mundane off our lists means never having to return to them, means consciously moving onto something else. Creating our own daily checkpoints puts us in full control of how the events of our day affect our leadership.

Make your checkpoint meaningful and attainable.

- Check in with a student, teacher, support staff, or cafeteria manager with whom you haven't spoken in a while

- Ask that first-time mom, recently back from maternity leave, how the baby is doing or if she needs anything
- Email the local police department to thank them for their help directing traffic during the recent snowstorm
- Thank a staff member for that book recommendation
- Stop into a classroom and compliment that teacher out loud in front of her class
- Call a parent to praise the growth of her child
- Tweet a picture of teachers being awesome or kids fully engaged
- Commit to one #bekind random act per day
- Play a game of knockout with the kids during recess
- Offer staff and students a mindfulness break through Calm.com ("Experience Calm")

Each of these, and so many like them, are so easy to let get away from us. Building in specific, attainable checkpoints provides us with a necessary measure of accomplishment, and they can make all the difference.

SAVING YOUR GAME

While checkpoints can provide us with signposts of our progress and can help us cross items off our lists, they are really only brief respites during our day. Sometimes it's imperative to commit to reaching a certain point before saving our game and hitting the power button. Because our academic year can feel like those early gaming days, interminable and without any tangible payoff in sight, saving our game allows us a necessary, if brief, breather during which we can reflect and recharge until we are ready to hit the power button again.

Thankfully, most academic calendars have at least three built-in save game points: a fall break, a winter holiday break, and a spring break. Make use of them. Knowing each is coming can help us focus on what we need to do in the interim, but saving our game during these breaks also should provide us time to think about what we *want* to do. In other words, saving our game affords us the time to step away from the mundane aspects of leadership, so we can focus on new, creative ways to lead. To return to the gaming analogy, if we save our game but don't reflect on the session that just ended, we are likely to make the same mistakes, fall for the same dastardly tricks, and fail again.

Of course, another vital benefit of saving our game is it allows us time away from the myriad pitfalls, seen and unseen, distractions, and boss battles we face each day. Making use of such time means posting a thoughtful away message to alert folks that, like them, you'll be enjoying this break and will respond to emails when you return. It means shutting down your laptop (even technology needs a save game) and unplugging from leadership for a few days. It means spending time with family and friends or taking that whirlwind trip you keep talking about. Because you've saved your game properly, everything that was present when you hit power, will still be there, unchanged, when you return.

Instead, it will be you that will return to your leadership changed because your save game allowed you to level up.

LEVEL UP LOCKER

As part of my commitment to saving my game, I will not even look at an email past 9pm. Though I have colleagues who use the evening to catch up on emails, I am all too aware of how my mind works, and to click on that red icon to check an email means committing to accepting whatever it says. Sometimes what it says makes that night's sleep an afterthought. In order to continue to level up, an evening email can wait until the morning.

During the summer, I stop what I'm doing at 2p, and even schedule meetings around that hour, and head over to Calm.com for a mindfulness retreat. Only ten minutes in length, the ambient sound of waves lapping against a shore coupled with the speaker's dulcet tone forces me to close my eyes and save my game. Those ten minutes are invaluable and have changed how I approach the rest of my day. Now, during the school year, I won't be able to plan for such a brain break, but I have a sticker affixed to a cabinet in front of my desk, which was given to me by a yoga instructor as a reminder to breathe. I look at it daily.

Use Google Calendar as a means of providing yourself with checkpoints. Plan them, put them on your calendar, and do your best to follow through with the checkpoint you provided yourself.

My wonderful predecessor left me a monthly to-do list when I took the position. She laid out, in painstaking detail, those items that had to be done in a given month regardless of what insinuated itself to the contrary. Each provided me with a checkpoint, an attainable goal I could see far in advance and meet when I was presented with it.

Consider taking a day in the summer and doing the same for yourself.

Before you save your game each day, make sure that doing so will allow you to start the next day from the same point. In other words, avoid bringing home anything that can wait until the next day, leave yourself sticky note reminders of the terrain you just traversed or of the most pressing thing that must get done upon your return. Saving your game is as mental as it is physical. If you only complete the latter, you haven't really saved your game at all.

13

RESTORING HEALTH

In most action-adventure games, our hero has a finite amount of health, which is reduced when he takes hits but can be replenished by health packs, energy drinks, or magic potions. Hovering over the main character's head like a menacing cloud, the health bar reminds gamers that, though fictitious, their vicarious counterparts get tired, feel pain, and sometimes need help. The way in which characters lose and gain health is up to the whimsy of the game developers, but, for the most part, each is largely unrealistic.

Take, for instance, our friend Mario. Though no health bar is present on screen, we know that there are basically two states of being before he dies. The first is his original form, small and spry but very weak. One touch by any enemy and he is donezo. The second, only slightly stronger version, is when Mario is large during which time he can withstand one touch from an enemy, which returns him to his original diminutive state. Clearly, both are unrealistic and meant to make the game more challenging.

On the other hand, but still as unrealistic, countless games allow the hero to take multiple shots, often by weapons like knives and guns, before they die. Because of the depth and breadth of such games, developers are wise to afford their main characters a more superhuman quality to offset the relative difficulty of the game. The aforementioned *Tomb Raider* is a perfect example. Ostensibly, a well-placed bullet or two should end Lara Croft's global spelunking. However, while she will die immediately if she falls from too high a jump, she is able to withstand an absurd amount of physical trauma before she loses her life. Unlike Mario, Lara has several opportunities to restore her health through packs, small and large, she can find and use along the way. All the while, her health bar remains a constant reminder of her mortality.

Health bar psychology is fascinating because it so often mirrors the gamer's personality. For instance, gamers who play each game with a devil-may-care attitude, moving at breakneck speed to beat the game, probably restore their health as quickly as possible, befitting of the pace at which they play the game. For the more cautious gamer, myself included, collecting and hoarding health packs is preferable because you never know when you're going to need them. In each case, it is likely that the gamer approaches his real life in the same way he approaches his vicarious life. So while gaming is often considered an escape, we are who we are regardless of the reality of our circumstance, landscape, or mission.

Consider, then, the parallels between our professional and personal lives as we approach our daily game in education. While we have to safeguard ourselves against too close a connection between the two, few of us enter our schools as one person and leave as a completely different person. In fact, our best teachers and leaders are masters at being authentic in everything they do, right up until it's time to put away that which is causing us personal pain so it does not affect our professional responsibilities. Though a precarious tightrope, it is one on which we must balance perpetually.

While it would be nice to have health packs dropped off to our room every time we feel like we're losing energy, in real life there are no cure-all remedies. Moreover, each of us is a distinct and different character in our own game, not a generic character meant to be played by others. In this way, we need to find or create our own health restoration methods in order to be near or at the top of our game as often as possible.

PRESS PAUSE

A common, if often mocked, cheat in gameplay is to push pause every time things get a little too overwhelming. When we see that monster approaching or have to time a difficult jump, pushing pause to stop the game and consider our next move is often necessary. While traditionalists will argue that takes away the spontaneity of the game and sullies the gamer's rep, most of us just want to play as well as possible as often as possible.

While we don't have the option to press pause literally on a difficult class or contentious summative evaluation, we can, and should, recognize when the path on which we headed needs to be reevaluated. Sometimes pressing pause just means calling out that which is weighing us down before agreeing to move on, together, in a way in which we hadn't intended but desperately need.

Remember that PD scenario I asked you to consider from both a first-person and a third-person perspective in "Point of View?"

As Chief Academic Officer of my K-12 district, I was in charge of professional development. In my four years, we moved from traditional "sit-and-get" PD to more collaborative, PLC-inspired PD. I am proud of our teachers who chose to level up, to lead or co-lead sessions, and to take steps toward lasting, positive change.

But last year we needed to push pause.

By February, staff in most of our schools are simply exhausted, and the winter months on the East coast are long, dark, and cold. Couple that with the fact that, at the secondary level, we simply tried to roll out too much in one year, and the staff stress level was palpable. As we began to plan for our full day PD, our supervisors and coaches argued that we needed to give time back to the teachers, to let them catch their breath, to push pause.

Like I said, deciding to push pause is one thing, but how we use that suspended reality is wholly different. Because I felt so responsible for so much of our staff's stress, I decided to call attention to it, en masse, and apologize. Through a short presentation, I told staff that sometimes we need to call out stress, by name, in order to take away its power. Whether that stress is imposed upon us or self-inflicted, without identifying it, we live under its spell.

Through a short, admittedly kitschy, activity, I asked staff, in teams, to finish a mad-lib inspired stress story. Using gifs and images representing what I knew caused us stress, teams filled in the blanks of the story I wrote, and the winning teams got a "jeans day" pass. At the end, I reiterated my apology for contributing to the collective stress and promised to work hard to relieve, not compound, such stress in the future.

But that wasn't enough.

The aforementioned supervisor and coach tandem had their own plan for pressing pause. And it was amazing. Through a bingo-style board, teachers could spend the last 75 minutes of the day doing what *they* wanted. With options like playing basketball in the gym, finding a quiet place to relax, working on class recommendations for next year, or writing a positive note to a colleague, teachers were on their own. And while the bingo game was a cool novelty, no one really cared about winning. In fact, for that short amount of time, no one really cared about *anything*.

To close the day, we invited teachers back to the cafeteria for one final surprise. After a brief affirmation of the power of pressing pause, each teacher was handed a personalized thank you note written by an administrator. Printed on garish orange paper for the world to see, every teacher walked away with a meaningful, if anonymous, reminder that they are appreciated and loved.

For five hours in the dead of winter, we decided to push pause. Though we don't walk around with our health bars hovering over our heads like in video games, I would guess that at the end of the day most of us were at full strength.

HITTING RESET

Sometimes we just need to start over.

Before memory cards and Sandisk flash drives, gamers were often forced to negotiate the current progress of their game with the chances they would be able to finish a game without having to start over. For instance, let's say you press start on a new game of *Super Mario Brothers* ready to save Princess Toadstool once and for all. You give yourself a little pep talk, make sure the lighting in the room is just right, and get to work. Then, even though you *know* the layout of each level with certainty, especially the first few, you inexplicably mistime a jump and end up in the abyss, down one life before your palms even get sweaty.

Now you're at an existential crossroads. Do you suck it up and press on without a full complement of lives or do you hit reset, start over, and give yourself that same little pep talk before beginning? For hardcore gamers, the former is the only way to go. There's pride in not hitting reset despite the fact that no one will ever know the difference. For the rest of us, giving ourselves every opportunity to defeat the game, even if it means having to start over, just makes sense.

Watching my five-year-old play *Super Mario Brothers*, which ultimately provided the impetus for *Level Up Leadership*, helps to illustrate this point with clarity. First of all, he loves Mario and everything associated with his bizarre, trippy adventures. Sometimes he'll speak in what he thinks is an Italian accent while he's playing. Last Halloween he dressed as Mario and then insisted on wearing the costume to pre-K on random days in say, March. By now, he has a handle on how to defeat the first few, basic levels, which never change.

Still, even equipped with all the knowledge and experience, he will sometimes make mistakes early in his gaming. For instance, on that first level, there are several, easy jumps over chasms that Mario has to navigate. None requires all that much dexterity or timing, and my son rarely makes mistakes on level one. He's played this level so many times that sometimes he'll narrate what's coming next and *still* mistime a jump or hit the A button instead of the B button and fall hopelessly to his 8-bit death. Immediately, he hops off the couch, runs to the console, and hits reset.

Why? Why does it matter that he lost a life so quickly? Because he rarely has the attention span or stamina to play for more than 10-15 minutes at a time, losing a life so early is inconsequential. But something in him demands that he start over because that last game wasn't his best.

Because he can't be bothered with perception or hubris, my man will hit reset all the time. In fact, we've talked about why it's important *not* to hit reset sometimes because it makes us focus that much harder when we know we have already made mistakes. Of course, those pearls of paternal wisdom are completely lost on him, but, hopefully, the premise of the advice will seep into his consciousness, applicable a little later in life.

Gamer's Journal: For me, hitting reset and restoring my health had more to do with coming to grips with my own anxiety than it did with finding a health pack or a magic potion. Before I knew what it was, I called the feeling "the dread," a palpable feeling of weight on the center of my chest. Though it never amounted to more than that singular physical symptom, I can't forget, and still struggle with, the mental manifestations of anxiety: sleeplessness (often on Sundays), song lyric repetition, conversation rehearsal, to name a few. Because I didn't know any better, I just sucked it up. This is how my brain works and this is who I am, I reasoned.

Then I met Karen Draper, my therapist for the last seven years. Within minutes of our first session, I knew something was going to change for me. After the requisite chit chat, we got down to business, and ultimately, she helped me understand that I suffer from anxiety with a side order of savior complex. The latter made sense to me because, I would argue, so many educators suffer from savior complex, a state of mind which convinces us that we have a duty to "save" those in our lives. The former really didn't come into focus until Karen introduced me to the "triangle": victim, rescuer, persecutor. Through her gifted and compassionate delivery, Karen illustrated how the triangle works and how I so often found myself playing one of the first two roles. If I wasn't helping those I meant to save, I was beating myself up for not being able to do so. And on and on it went.

There is no magic potion for my anxiety, though Lexapro is at least a distant cousin, and that's okay. In this case, I had to level up my personal life. I had to accept that I wasn't able to make sense of how my mind worked, and I needed help. Karen provided me with an entirely different kind of walkthrough: one about me but written by someone else.

Now, think about hitting reset in your current role. And, to be clear, hitting reset, in gaming and in leadership, isn't necessarily akin to quitting. In fact, it's quite the opposite. Choosing to hit reset on a game, on a lesson, on a strategy, just means you have the self-awareness to know that, if given the opportunity to begin again, you know you can do better.

Teachers, the really good ones anyway, are constantly asked to hit reset. In fact, they may do so several times in the same *class period*. Recognizing a lesson isn't going well, despite meticulous planning and preparation, is as humbling an experience as a teacher can have. She has to make peace with the fact that she needs to hit reset, do so, and then somehow move on with her lesson all in what amounts to a few minutes of real time.

Leaders, the really good ones anyway, are constantly asked to hit reset. Recognizing a professional development plan didn't work, accepting that what's important to us may not be important to our team, and questioning why we made certain decisions are all part of the reflective nature of leveling up.

Like Mario falling into that abyss over and over again, sometimes we just need to hit reset.

LEVEL UP LOCKER

Though I'm still working on the mechanics of my own health restoration, it is imperative to step away from our professional lives every day. Whether you're a compulsive planner and budget the same time every day or you have some sort of mnemonic device to remind you to stop working, the first step in restoring your health is recognizing that it's getting low.

When I moved from central office to the principalship, I was organizing my new office and came across "stress relieving hand sanitizer." Rolling my eyes at its multi-purpose marketing, I squirted some into my hands anyway. For hours, I could smell the admittedly relaxing scent on my hands, and I felt energized. Maybe I'm just a schlub who fell for it, but I certainly felt restored that afternoon. Find that what gives you instant gratification and make it a priority. For some, that could be popping on some Krishna Das ("Krishna Das Music") and zoning out to his mesmerizing chants. For others, it might be heading into a darkened gym and shooting hoops for ten minutes. For still others, it's a planned, slow-sipping cup of coffee. Regardless of your muse or medium, self-care is health restoration, and it's simply too vital to ignore.

Make the weekends and days off meaningful. As the father of two small children, I know how outlandish this sounds. Oftentimes my wife and I are more exhausted on Sunday night than on any other night of the week. Still, that fatigue is absent of SGOs, parent phone calls, and state audits. Perhaps we can consider two health bars hovering over our heads: a professional and a personal. So while our personal health bar is on life support, we are ready to attack Monday because our professional health bar is at 100%.

A friend once said to me, "If I'm ever having a bad day, I just go right to kindergarten." Like our gaming alter egos, health restoration is all around us. Head down to kindergarten, sit on the carpet crisscross-applesauce, read with the kids, let them ramble about dinosaurs and their mommy's new shoes. If only for a few minutes, we shed that which is weighing us down in favor of runny noses and nonsequiturs.

I often find that a heavy dose of stress is mitigated by a random act of kindness. Maybe it's not even so random. Similar to the feeling we get when we watch a loved one open a gift we bought for them, experiencing or causing someone's else's joy somehow deflates our own stress if only for a moment. While we inevitably return to whatever it was that was causing our stress, it is rendered powerless temporarily while we provide someone else with a reason to smile. Then, our health bar has been restored, even slightly, as we return to our routine.

14

HIGH SCORE

For years, the true mark of any gamer was to find his name atop the high score list, the leaderboard. Etching his initials next to that score for the world to see provided a euphoric, if not narcissistic, reminder to the world of that gamer's place in the pantheon of (insert game) excellence. Because early iterations of gaming titles didn't include a finite end, gamers knew they couldn't "beat" the game, so competition came in the form of beating a personal high score and in beating the posted high scored of gamers that came before. Typically in the form of a top ten, high scores served as the backdrop of idling games, patiently waiting for their next quarter. They were an advertisement, a challenge, a chance for immortality.

In a classic episode of *Seinfeld* (David and Seinfeld), Jerry and George find themselves back at the pizza shop in their old neighborhood. Awaiting them is the same game of *Frogger* ("Frogger"), the classic arcade game in which you control a frog trying to make its way across an impossibly busy highway, for which George once held the high score. Like a moth to a flame, George wanders over to the game only to find that his high score still remains atop the leaderboard. In typical *Seinfeld* fashion, the rest of the episode is devoted to George's absurd mission to secure the game for himself, making it impossible for anyone to beat his high score. Though farcical, George's obsession with maintaining the high score is representative of gaming culture's fascination with its own superiority.

The irony, of course, is that the only way for gamers to truly revel in their greatness is to reveal themselves as the human embodiment of those initials. And when they do, to whom does that score really matter? With whom are they actually competing?

The 2007 documentary *The King of Kong: A Fistful of Quarters* (Gordon), which could easily be mistaken for a mockumentary produced by Fred Armisen and Bill Hader, explores the extraordinary lengths to which gamers go to secure their place in gaming lore. Billy Mitchell, a score-obsessed narcissist, holds several gaming scoring records, including for the classic, and very difficult, *Donkey Kong*. A shameless self-promoter, Mitchell reminds the audience time and again how dominant a player he was, particularly during the 1980s. Meanwhile, laid-off engineer and lovable loser Steve Wiebe decides to embark on his own quest for video game immortality, taking aim at Mitchell's *Kong* record. What unfolds is a truly sad and absurd game of tug-of-war over high scores, ego, and integrity. Without providing further spoilers, the documentary provides a relevant and poignant analogy to education's increasingly score-obsessed evaluation culture.

Before Charlotte Danielson ("Charlotte Danielson Group") and Robert Marzano (Marzano Research), education's equivalent of Mitchell and Wiebe, before domains, components, and indicators, before shaded boxes and Student Growth Percentiles (SGPs), teacher evaluations were much simpler. And that's not to suggest that such simplicity is synonymous with superiority. Rather, evaluations were meticulously scrawled, narratively based snapshots of whatever moment in time a leader chose to perform the observation. Depending on the evaluator, the notes for a given observation could go on for pages, the feedback for which could rival a common novella.

In many ways, "old school" evaluations were far more difficult for the observer. Consider that the observer had to write everything that happened during the lesson, had to be mindful to remain objective during such note taking, had to eventually type those notes up formally, had to leave room for meaningful commendations and recommendations, and had to meet with his teacher to go through it all. Forget the fact that leaders come from all kinds of content backgrounds, so the narrative and feedback given by a former English teacher is going to look and function differently than that of a less writing-intensive content area.

Still, there was something about reading that narrative assessment of your work that felt more genuine, more connected to the observer. Sure, modern evaluation rubrics still have places for narrative recommendations and commendations, but the scope of each is dwarfed by the packaged, generic language decided upon by people we've never met. Scores were more meaningful, for better or for worse, when determined by the commentary of a colleague rather than by the language of an educational "expert."

Of course, it would be foolish to pine for the nostalgia of such evaluation practices without considering its flaws.

Because accountability and tenure reform were mere whispers at the time, evaluations didn't carry the weight of an omnipotent oversight tied to continued employment the way it does today. As such, we have to wonder how driven quality teachers were to continue to grow if they knew they were working in the relative comfort and safety of tenure. Without scores attached to their names and to their employment, teachers had little extrinsic motivation to get better if they were constantly being told they were "proficient" or "meeting expectations" without any common language to illustrate what such distinctions meant.

Enter Charlotte Danielson and Robert Marzano.

For the first time, teachers would be evaluated based on an exhaustive system replete with domains, components, indicators, and common language. While each framework preaches the importance of quality teaching across grade levels and content areas, each creates a teaching "leaderboard" not unlike we would see from our favorite video game. Obviously, among the many differences between teacher evaluation and video game high scores, the former should be kept between the teacher and her supervisor; the latter is posted for the world to see, often in loud, ostentatious color and font. Advocates for the Danielson and Marzano frameworks will argue that common language levels the instructional playing field and provides transparency for teachers and administrators. Detractors will argue that, like we often bemoan of our students' reaction to graded work, our work, which is so complex and multi-faceted, shouldn't be whittled down to a final, quantifiable score.

Let's return, then, to our *King of Kong* adversaries. Billy Mitchell achieved the game's top score, sat on it, and let everyone with a passing interest in gaming know that he was, in fact, the king of *Donkey Kong*. Steve Wiebe went to great lengths to surpass Mitchell's high score, and when he did, Mitchell went to even greater lengths to disprove the feat. In effect, these two strangers with a similar interest in gaming, pit themselves against each other on a decades-long, largely meaningless pursuit of a high score on a video game. Both would eventually fade into obscurity, if not irrelevance, if not for the 2007 documentary dedicated to their obsession with a high score. Even then, each is a pop culture trivia answer at best, but they also represent our culture's fixation on scores and competition.

Now, consider your school's Mitchell and Wiebe. Think about how your high scorers wear their 4s and "distinguished" labels as badges of honor, perhaps going so far as to form "clubs" in their own glory. Then think about those teachers who are consistently consistent, never going above or below that which is considered "proficient." Even further, think about those teachers who do fall below "proficient," who demonstrate a real need for support, who may not be long for this profession.

Level Up Leadership
Brian Kulak

Gamer's Journal: My high score is 2004, and it will never change.

During my sixth year in the classroom, I had finally hit my stride. I had cemented myself as the "senior specialist," boasting a schedule specific to seniors, save for some high-flying underclassmen in my journalism class. I was trying things in class that either brought raised eyebrows or gleeful smiles, depending on the audience. I had had three books--Tom Perrotta's Joe College (2006), Tawni O'Dell's Back Roads (2004), and Joanna Hershon's Swimming (2002)-- removed from the curriculum for reasons I still can't fathom. I had developed a public speaking activity called "The Hot Seat" of which I was very proud and still use today with my fifth graders. And I got to spend every day with what would become my favorite class, the Audubon High School Class of 2004.

Each of us has a favorite class, a group of kids with whom we just click, with whom we laugh more often than not, and with whom we keep in contact long after graduation. This group was so special that it didn't take me long to recognize them as such, and I believe that when I did, they knew it. From that point on, we experienced senior year together. I taught them how to read, write, and speak like college students; they taught me how to teach them better. At the end of the year, we planned a Senior Field Day, the first and last of its kind, which was run almost entirely by the kids. Meant to model a collegiate field day, minus the binge drinking obviously, we flipped burgers, played wiffle ball, had a dunk tank, and enjoyed a student garage band concert. Every so often, I'll go back to pictures I kept from that day and marvel at how close we were.

Consider this: the shortstop on my men's team is from the class of 2004, a contributor to my blog is from the class of 2004, I was an official taster for a new brewery opened by a member of the class of 2004, the only class reunion to which I was invited personally was the class of 2004. There are more examples, more small moments, more inside jokes from that year, but when I reflect of my career, I'll see the number 2004 blinking in red lights.

They are my high score.

Do our teachers' "high score" define, cluster, empower or deflate them? Are most of our teachers Mitchells or Wiebes?

One of the most challenging aspects of our score-obsessed evaluation is convincing teachers that any score in any domain only represents a snapshot of their overall practice. Scoring well in any domain is as fleeting as scoring poorly. In this way, considering teachers through a numerical lens, or allowing teachers to view themselves through that lens, does little to increase capacity, encourage growth, or engender the kind of collaboration we so desperately need from our teachers. In effect, it creates a culture of Mitchells.

While we may never find a perfect balance between bureaucratic, numerically-based and substantive, narratively-based evaluation, it is imperative that we overtly and clearly communicate with our staff our desire to help them grow. In fact, to go a step further, we need to communicate our desire to grow along with them. In order to offset the ever-present us vs. them mentality, we need to elicit, if not at least consider, feedback on our leadership from the very people we mean to lead. Holding a mirror up to our own leadership as we consider the feedback we craft for our teachers both validates the feedback we do provide, and forces us to be as reflective of our leadership practice as we ask our teachers to be about their instructional practice.

Unlike Mitchell and Wiebe, most teachers aren't in competition with each other, even if they demonstrate a flippant or off-handed response to the contrary. They are, however, in competition with their best self, with their last evaluation. Tapping into an often-innate competitiveness, level up leaders use evaluations and their requisite feedback as a means of posting teachers' high scores in a way that challenges them to *want* to beat those scores. Rather than generic, copy and paste feedback, level up leaders consider their words thoughtfully, craft their suggestions for growth carefully, and celebrate teachers genuinely. Doing so proves to teachers that we are as invested in their growth as we expect them to be. Then, perhaps, we can convince teachers that any high score is as fleeting as the lesson to which it is attached, but like any video game, we can always hit reset and try again.

LEVEL UP LOCKER

Start each year by preaching your insistence on providing actionable feedback. Show staff examples of what they can expect from your narrative, and before long, teachers will scroll first to that section before even considering the highlighted numbers in reference to their performance.

Create a faux evaluation for yourself or ask a trusted teacher to help with it. Model the kind of reflection you want from them. If you struggle with a certain domain (for me, it's "operations and management"), score yourself at a 1 or a 2 and show staff. Then hammer home the point that you're aware of the areas in which you struggle, you're committed to improving, and you'd love their help.

Reach out to members of your leadership team and find out who considers herself an expert feedback provider. Then, encourage that volunteer to present on feedback during an upcoming district administrative meeting. Too often, folks just don't know they aren't very good at providing feedback because teachers are unlikely to tell them and they don't have access to everyone else's feedback. Change that and train your team to provide consistent feedback. Teachers will appreciate it, instruction and management practices will improve, and your culture will be built on mutual trust.

Turn evaluation scores and rubrics into fun ways to "score" each other in other areas. Give the "staff mom" (every staff has one) a 4 for always remembering everyone's birthday. Give your amazing secretary a 4 for keeping the building from falling apart. Give the staff jokester a 4 for always making you laugh. Look, create as many silly categories as you want, but if we can somehow change the perception of the actual number, perhaps folks will stop worrying about which numbers end up next to their names.

Always consider your words against what you would want or expect when you were in the classroom. We've all had leaders from whom we've learned simply by breathing the same air and other from whom we've learned to remember to keep our fire drill route prominently displayed. As a leader, you are an amalgam of every leader with whom you've ever worked, so it's imperative that you remember that you were a teacher first as you craft your evaluation feedback.

15

THE FINAL LEVEL

Video game final levels, regardless of the console, generation, or genre, tend to take on a similar personality. There's a palpable intensity, often exacerbated by a frenetic pace and ominous music. We can assume the gamer's palms sweat, his heart rate picks up, and the pressure he puts on himself to succeed is only mitigated by the possibility of gaming glory. We know he has made countless mistakes on his journey, he may have read the walkthrough, and he may have thrown his controller once or twice. But make no mistake, the end is nigh.

As Mario stands on the precipice of his own glory, he, too, is forced to reflect. He wonders into how many chasms had he fallen? How many stray hammers bonked him back to the beginning of a level? How many mistimed jumps, overly aggressive maneuvers, or errant fireballs separated him from his long, lost princess? His journey has been long, repetitive, and humbling, but it's almost over.

When Mario finally executes the perfect combination of moves to defeat Bowser and save Princess Toadstool, the once ominous music is replaced by a triumphant ditty, and a frankly underwhelming reunion between the two lovebirds commences. As the music plays on, Mario is offered the option to play another level; the reward for his painstaking journey is another journey. Still, Mario used everything he learned from the combined failures of his past to complete his mission and save the princess.

Like Mario, we, too, are provided with an option to play another level at the beginning of every school year. For us, little is the same from game to game. Sure, we enter the same doors, are greeted by the same colleagues, and are aware of our general surroundings, but we cannot predict the pitfalls or triumphs of the year ahead. In fact, it is likely that *we* changed more than the landscape to which we return.

Leveling up should not be a ceiling to which we aspire. In fact, we are better served to imagine that ceiling continuing to float just out of reach, that high score a constant reminder of how we can improve, if even by a single point. Rather, leveling up should serve as a mantra, a game within the game, a personal challenge. You've already leveled up countless times in your career, and I can prove it.

Reflect on year one in the classroom or as a leader. Think meaningfully about all the myriad things you didn't yet know, that you couldn't possibly know. Then think about how many mistakes you made in just that year, how many opportunities to grow and connect with others you missed, and how many times you doubted yourself and your path. Have you leveled up since then? Of course, you have. That's the easy part.

Now run through the same exercise, only this time consider it in reference to *last year*. Is the list similar? Have the issues on which you reflect changed? Do you find yourself with more answers than questions?

Ultimately, leveling up isn't a destination; it's a state of being. It's a perpetually reflective way to ensure that you are committed to growth and improvement. Each year your cast of characters changes, even slightly, so the game you play is never quite the same. Each year is an opportunity to connect with new students, to strengthen relationships with colleagues. Each year provides a finite ending point, but the path on which you travel is up to you.

So cue the theme music. Grab a controller. Seek out Easter eggs and use the walkthrough. Better yet: *create*

Easter eggs and *write* the walkthrough. Post a new high score.

Your EduGame is constantly evolving and so are you.

LEVEL UP LOCKER

Start small. Like in gaming, we need to figure out ourselves before we can determine how to level up. Think meaningfully about who you are, what your "thing" is, and how you can level up. If you're a literacy maven, level up by offering to run a workshop for colleagues. If math is your jam, create and post fun equations around your building. Make clear to your staff and to your kids that you are constantly leveling up. Then, watch as folks get excited to join you.

Create a level up tribe in your school or district. The gaming community is tightly knit and, though competitive, protective of itself. Education is very similar; we all want to be the best we can be, but we recognize the importance other people play in our careers. Be vulnerable and seek out EduGamers. Who seems on the cutting edge of instruction and professional development? Who always has great ideas at faculty meetings or at happy hour? Maybe the person is you, but in order to level up, it's imperative that you invite others to play.

Reflect on the walkthrough chapter. Educators tend to be reflective by nature, so they are constantly thinking about their practice. Imagine, then, spending time writing down how you arrived at an instructional decision, providing a step-by-step guide for yourself. You may only do this a couple times a year, but when you do, offer it to colleagues via a tweet, group email, or brief presentation at a faculty meeting. If even one colleague takes you up on it, you've invited her into your tribe, and you've both leveled up.

Speaking of Twitter, use the hashtag #leveluplead when you level up.

Building an online cache of strategies, activities, and support will only encourage others to level up.

Don't stop. At 42, I'm entering my 20th year in education, and while I shudder to think about the teacher I was at 22 and the leader I was at 37, I recognize how much more room I have to grow. We all do. There's something special happening in education right now. While folks outside the arena are making ill-advised decisions based on scatter plots and bottom lines, the people inside the arena are transforming the field one idea, one tweet, one book at a time. We know how important our work is, and we believe in each other and in our kids. Again, leveling up isn't a destination; it's a decision, a commitment, a promise.

Player 1: Push start and level up.

Gamer's Journal: While the idea for Level Up Leadership came to me in a revelatory way, the motivation to write a book can be attributed to two people: Dan Whalen (@whalen) and Rich Czyz (@RACzyz).

Dan was mentioned a few times in this book and is one of the most positive people I've ever met. So positive, in fact, that he started a hashtag at our high school, #chsonegoodthing, that encouraged our school community to tweet one positive picture, idea, or shout out per day. The result was a windfall of positivity from which the high school is still benefitting. He also commits to a new venture, a new goal every year. After living through his annual goals with him, albeit from the sidelines, for four years, I finally decided to commit to my own. On January 2, 2018, I began my daily routine from which I have not wavered: wake up and write at 5a, head to the gym at 6a, and begin my day at 7a. I'd like to think I would have arrived at this schedule on my own, but I know that because of Dan, I created my own one good thing.

Rich is the author of *The 4 O'Clock Faculty: A Rogue Guide to Revolutionizing Professional Development* (Czyz). After I read his book, which mirrored so closely to my own philosophy on PD, I took a shot and reached out to him. I knew he was from New Jersey, I knew I wanted to pick his brain, and I knew that his advice would be sage. He responded and agreed immediately. Now, just for context, this is a man who has built a reputation as a leading voice in education, who has seen his Twitter follows top 14K, and who, at the time, was a primary school principal. Still, after answering several questions via email, he offered to meet in person. Weeks later, on a chilly winter afternoon, Rich walked me through his writing routine, his publication process, and his leadership philosophy. We met for over an hour on January 19th, 2018. In May, I finished my initial draft. In August, I signed my first ever book deal. Again, I'd like to think this all would have happened without Rich, but I know that because of him, my life changed. That's why I asked him to write the foreword, and in true Rich fashion, he agreed with grace and humility.

Thank you to my first two Level Up Leaders, Dan and Rich.

WORKS CITED

Adventure. Atari, 1980.

Aslam, Salman. "Twitter by the Numbers (2018): Stats, Demographics & Fun Facts." 18 Sept. 2018, www.omnicoreagency.com/twitter-statistics/.

Asteroids. Atari, 1979.

AtariAge. 1998, www.atariage.com/2600/.

Benioff, David and D.B.Weiss, creators. *Game of Thrones.* HBO, 2011.

Breakout EDU. 2016, www.breakoutedu.com/.

Brinks, Melissa. "The Controversial Story Behind the First Easter Egg in Video Game History." Ranker, 2018, www.ranker.com/list/first-video-game-easter-egg-atari-2600-adventure/melissa-brinks.

Brooker, Charlie, creator. *Black Mirror.* Netflix, 2011.

Burgess, Dave. *Teach Like a Pirate: Increase Student Engagement, Boost Your Creativity, and Transform Your Life as an Educator.* Dave Burgess Consulting, Inc., 2012.

Calm. 2012, www.calm.com/.

Carroll, Lewis. *Alice's Adventures in Wonderland.* MacMillan, 1865.

Charlotte Danielson Group. 2017, www.danielsongroup.org/charlotte -danielson/.

ColecoVision. Coleco, 1982.

Commodore 64. Commodore International, 1982.

Contra. Konami, 1987.

Czyz, Rich. *The Four O'Clock Faculty: A Rogue Guide to Revolutionizing Professional Development.* Dave Burgess Consulting, 2017.

Dan, Phan Nguyen Khanh. *Resident Evil: Director's Cut - Walkthrough/FAQ,* 2001, https://www.ign.com/faqs/2003/

resident-evil-directors-cut-
walkthroughfaq-381944

David, Larry and Jerry Seinfeld,
    creators. *Seinfeld.* NBC, 1989.

Dig Dug. Namco, 1982.

Donkey Kong. Nintendo, 1981.

Doom. ID Software, 1993.

Edcamp. www.edcamp.org/.

Edutopia. George Lucas Educational
    Foundation, 1991,
    www.edutopia.org/.

The Edvocate. 2018,
    www.theedadvocate.org/.

Escape the Room.
    www.escapetheroom.com/.

Flipgrid. www.flipgrid.com/.

Frogger. Sega, 1981.

Gilligan, Vince, creator. *Breaking Bad.*
    High Bridge Productions, 2008.

Gonzalez, Jennifer. *Cult of Pedagogy.*
    2018, www.cultofpedagogy.com/.

Gordon, Seth, director. *The King of Kong: A Fistful of Quarters*. LargeLab, 2008.

G Suite for K12 Institutions. 2016, www.edu.google.com/k-12-solutions/g-suite/?modal_active=none.

Haggis, Paul, director. *Crash*. Bob Yari Productions, 2004.

Hershon, Joanna. *Swimming*. Ballantine Books, 2002.

Intellivision. Mattel Electronics, 1979.

Ironsword: Wizards and Warriors II. Zippo Games, 1989.

Jean-Marie, G., & Martinez, A. (2007). Race, gender, & leadership: Perspectives of female secondary leaders. In S. M. Nielsen & M. S. Plakhotnik (Eds.), Proceedings of the Sixth Annual College of Education Research Conference: Urban and International Education Section (pp. 43-48). Miami: Florida International University.

http://coeweb.fiu.edu/research_c
onference/

"John Marston." *Red Dead Wiki*,
www.reddead.wikia.com/wiki/Joh
n_Marston.

Judge, Mike, director. *Office Space*. 20th
Century Fox, 1999.

Kohler, Chris. "Oct. 18, 1985: Nintendo
Entertainment System Launches."
Wired, 14 Jan. 2018,
www.wired.com/2010/10/1018ni
ntendo-nes-launches/.

Krishna Das Music. 2018,
www.krishnadas.com/.

Kulak, Brian. "Building Staff Rapport
with Flash Lessons." *Edutopia*, 26
Apr. 2016,
www.edutopia.org/blog/building-
staff-rapport-flash-lessons-brian-
kulak.

"Leon Scott Kennedy." Resident Evil
Wiki,
www.residentevil.wikia.com/wiki/
Leon_Scott_Kennedy.

The Legend of Zelda. Nintendo, 1986.

Level Up Leadership: Advance Your EduGame. 2018, www.leveluplead.com/.

"List of Voxer Groups." *The EdSquad.* 2017, www.theedsquad.org/voxer.

Miller, Monica K, and Alicia Summers. "Gender Differences in Video Game Characters' Roles, Appearances, and Attire as Portrayed in Video Game Magazines." *Sex Roles,* 18 Sept. 2007, pp. 733–742.

Madden NFL. EA Sports, 1988.

Minecraft. Mojang, 2009.

Nintendo Entertainment System. Nintendo, 1985.

Nintendo Entertainment System: NES Classic Edition - Official Site. 2018, www.nintendo.com/nes-classic/.

The Noun Project. 2010, www.thenounproject.com/.

O'Dell, Tawni. *Back Roads*. New American Library, 2004.

Milestone, Lewis, director. *Ocean's Eleven*. Dorchester Productions, 1960.

Pac-Man. Namco, 1980.
Paperboy. Atari Games, 1985.

Perrotta, Tom. *Joe College*. St. Martin's Griffin, 2006.

PlayStation (Console). Sony, 1995.

Pong. Atari, 1972.

Rampage. Bally Midway, 1986.

Resident Evil. Capcom, 1996.

Marzano Research | Becoming a Reflective Teacher. 2018, www.marzanoresearch.com/robert-j-marzano.

"Schools and Staffing Survey (SASS)." *National Center for Education Statistics (NCES) Home Page, a Part of the U.S. Department of Education, National Center for Education Statistics*, 2004,

www.nces.ed.gov/surveys/sass/ta
bles/sass0304_001_p1s.asp.

Sega Genesis. Sega, 1989.

Silent Hill. Konami, 1999.

Space Invaders. Midway, 1978.

Super Mario Brothers. Nintendo, 1985.

Super Nintendo Entertainment System.
Nintendo, 1991.

TeacherTube, 2018,
www.teachertube.com/.

TED: Ideas Worth Spreading, 2018,
www.ted.com/talks.

Tomb Raider. Core Design, 1996.

TweetDeck. 2008,
www.tweetdeck.twitter.com/.

Voxer. 2018, www.voxer.com/.

Wizards and Warriors. Rare, 1987.

Wolfenstein 3D. ID Software, 1992.

Zorrilla, Michele. "Video Games and
Gender: Game Representation."

Level Up Leadership
Brian Kulak

Video Games and Gender, 2011,
www.radford.edu/~mzorrilla2/the
sis/gamerepresentation.html.

OTHER EDUMATCH BOOKS

In this collaborative project, twenty educators located throughout the United States share educational strategies that have worked well for them, both with students and in their professional practice.

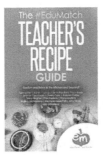

Hey there, awesome educator! We know how busy you are. Trust us, we get it. Dive in as fourteen international educators share their recipes for success, both literally and metaphorically! In this book, we come together to support one another not only in the classroom, but also in the kitchen.

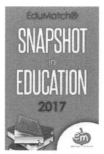

We're back! EduMatch proudly presents Snapshot in Education (2017). In this two-volume collection, 32 educators and one student share their tips for the classroom and professional practice. Topics include culture, standards, PBL, instructional models, perseverance, equity, PLN, and more.

This book started as a series of separate writing pieces that were eventually woven together to form a fabric called The Y in You. The question is, "What's the 'why' in you?" Why do you? Why would you? Why should you? Through the pages in this book, you will gain the confidence to be you, and understand the very power in what being you can produce.

Follow the Teacher's Journey with Brian as he weaves together the stories of seven incredible educators. Each step encourages educators at any level to reflect, grow, and connect. The Teacher's Journey will ignite your mind and heart through its practical ideas and vulnerable storytelling.

Adversity itself is not what defines us. It is how we react to that adversity and the choices we make that creates who we are and how we will persevere. The Fire Within: Lessons from defeat that have ignited a passion for learning is a compilation of stories from amazing educators who have faced personal adversity head on and have become stronger people for it. They use their new-found strength to support the students and teachers they work with.

This book challenges the thought that "teaching" begins only after certification and college graduation. Instead, it describes how students in teacher preparation programs have value to offer their future colleagues, even as they are learning to be teachers! This book provides positive examples, helpful tools, and plenty of encouragement for preservice teachers to learn, to dream, and to do.

The maker mindset sets the stage for the Fourth Industrial Revolution, empowering educators to guide their students to pursue a path of learning that is meaningful to them. Addressing a shifting culture in today's classrooms, we look to scaling up and infusing this vision in a classroom, in a school, and even in a district.

The concept of being innovative can be made to sound so simple. We think of a new idea. We take a risk and implement the new idea. We fail, learn, and move forward. But what if the development of the innovative thinking isn't the only roadblock? What if so much of your day is spent solving the issues around you that even the attempt at developing new ideas is not even on your radar? What if you long to have more divergent teachers in your school district or to be that divergent teacher, but you simply don't know where to start?

EduMatch® is back for our third annual Snapshot in Education. Dive in as 21 educators share a snapshot of what they learned, what they did, and how they grew in 2018. Topics include purpose, instructional strategies, equity, cultural competence, education technology, and much more!

educational matchmaker

51333156R00157

Made in the USA
Columbia, SC
16 February 2019